Peter Alliss was born into golf. The height of his playing career came in 1958, when he won the Italian, Spanish and Portuguese Opens in three successive weeks. Today, he is the doyen of golf commentators and as such is regarded as the rightful heir to Henry Longhurst. His television programmes *Around with Alliss* and *Pro-Celebrity Golf* are the most popular of their kind. His previous books include *Bedside Golf, More Bedside Golf* and *An Autobiography,* all available in Fontana.

'I believe that the highest achievement of the golf instructor may not be in teaching but in getting the pupil to learn'
TOMMY ARMOUR

Professional (at Indoor School of Golf): 'Are you going to have a lesson, Madam?'
Madam: 'No, but my friend is, I learnt last week.'

PLAY GOLF
with
PETER ALLISS

In collaboration with Renton Laidlaw
Edited by Gordon Menzies

Fontana/Collins

Contents

Foreword by Renton Laidlaw

First published by BBC Publications 1977
Revised edition first published by Willow Books 1983
First issued in Fontana Paperbacks 1986

Made by Lennard Books
Mackerye End
Harpenden, Herts AL5 5DR
Designed by David Pocknell's Company Ltd
Production Reynolds Clark Associates Ltd
Printed and bound in Great Britain
by William Collins Sons & Co. Ltd, Glasgow

FOREWORD

by Renton Laidlaw, Golf Correspondent, The Standard

It was inevitable that Peter Alliss would choose golf as his career and equally certain that he would be a tremendous success.

Alliss was born into the game in 1931 in Berlin where his father Percy was professional, and his immense natural talent as golfer and his extrovert personality have helped him to a succession of triumphs on and off the course. Just as he was a stylish golfer so his performances as a golfing commentator on television are equally eloquent.

He made his debut in top-line golf at the precocious age of sixteen when he played in the Open Championship of 1947, won by Fred Daly at Hoylake. In the ensuing 23 years he was to win twenty-two major tournaments, in Britain, Europe and as far afield as Brazil.

During his tournament career he emerged as one of Britain's most colourful and, on occasion, controversial characters. Once he refused to defend his P.G.A. title because he was already committed to taking part in a televised challenge game in Tobago – an incident which typically illustrates his always independent spirit.

His forthright manner frequently got him into trouble in the early days with the 'establishment'. He was golf's 'angry young man' of the fifties, attempting almost single-handed to get a better deal for the tournament professionals in opposition to the old timers who saw change as an unnecessary evil that could be avoided.

His crusade was frustrated then but twenty years later that better deal for which Alliss had fought so hard became a reality with the formation of an independent tournament players section operating under the umbrella of the Professional Golfers' Association.

A former captain of the P.G.A., Alliss first played in the Ryder Cup against the Americans in 1953 at Wentworth when, in the singles, he lost on the last green to Willie Turnesa after having been ahead in the closing stages. It was a defeat which had a traumatic effect on the then 22-year-old Alliss until he wiped out the memory with some of the finest Ryder Cup performances in the history of the match.

His one hole victory over Arnold Palmer in the 1963 Cup match at Atlanta when Palmer was at the peak of his career must rate as one of Alliss' greatest achievements in golf. That win was his personal rejoinder to Palmer's exhortation to the American team on the eve of the match that there were not ten men in the world who could hope to beat the Americans! Few players have struck the golf ball better than Alliss, who left the circuit in 1969 to widen the scope of his activities in the game which has always been in his blood.

Turning his back on tournament play was not so surprising. The British circuit, in itself, was hardly enough to satisfy, or to stretch the huge talent of the man. The fact that he is jack of all trades and unlike the old proverb, master of most, has always meant that he has needed a number of outlets in which to channel his great drive and energy.

He has a sort of love-hate relationship with the game which, he will admit readily enough, has given him great joy and some heartaches. The changes he has made in recent years have, fortunately for the rest of us, enabled him to stay on the golfing scene without having to experience the ludicrous pain of facing up to a two-foot putt.

Indeed, it makes him appreciate even more the great talent of those American golfers and some British players as well who can bravely hole out across bumpy greens in the cold chill of evening to make half-way cuts and reasonable cheques – much more reasonable nowadays than when he was an active competitor.

Apart from his charm Peter has that great golfing asset, a sense of

humour. His gleaming blue Rolls Royce sports a number plate – PUT 3 – that cocks a snook at all those armchair critics.

When he gave up the circuit – a difficult decision made all the more easy for him because of that putting twitch – he was only 39, but a new life, a much more lucrative life, began for him at 40.

Whether it was the putting problems in themselves or the fact that his many and varied interests prevented him from spending enough time to beat the problem, Alliss only occasionally regrets missing out on the excitement of competing at top level.

When television chiefs realised that top line golf produced excellent viewing Alliss was in on the ground floor, a natural number two to the late Henry Longhurst. The rapport established between the doyen of golfing journalists and Alliss provided the ideal reporting blend. Now Alliss is as much in demand in America for television engagements as he is in Britain – and not always for his commentaries.

Over the years he has built up a reputation as a teacher of golf, believing that the game should be kept as simple as possible. Not for Alliss complicated technique, but a straightforward, easy to understand, approach which was fascinatingly revealed in the 'Play Golf' series he made in Scotland for the BBC.

If Alliss and Longhurst teamed up perfectly on the television front, Alliss found another perfect partnership in golf architecture with his golfing chum, Dave Thomas. Today the Alliss–Thomas partnership is respected throughout the world. It was their firm that the Royal and Ancient Golf Club of St Andrews called in when alterations and changes were needed for the Turnberry course when it hosted the 1977 Open Championship.

From his luxury home near Hindhead in Surrey Alliss jets around the world to keep exhibition, teaching, television, lecture and course design dates. Golf has been good for Peter Alliss and Alliss has been good for golf. He still has personal 'Everests' to conquer. One day, perhaps, he will be asked to captain the Ryder Cup team – sooner maybe than later – and he will do that well, tempering that apparently effortless style and ready smile with requisite touches of aggression and determination.

This book is as lively and as entertaining as the man's career. It is not difficult because Peter Alliss never found the game of golf to be difficult. If you want intricate theorising on golf's complexities do not go any further. If you want simple, honest to goodness advice, 'Play Golf' is the book for you.

GETTING TO GRIPS

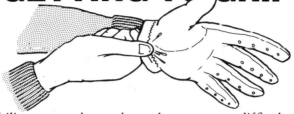

Prince Philip suggested once that polo was a more difficult game to play than golf because in polo you are trying to hit a moving ball while riding a horse! In all fairness I think he's wrong. Golf must be the most difficult game to start from scratch.

Why? For one thing the swing is unnatural and the complicated technique – sometimes over-complicated by golfers themselves – can only be perfected by regular time-consuming effort-demanding practice. That's the challenge.

Progress can be slow, at first, but once you have trained your muscles to react almost instinctively and have stopped slicing into the rough, hooking into the woods, fluffing your wedges and thinning your irons you will find golf an irresistible challenge.

Don't expect to become a Jack Nicklaus overnight because you will probably never ever come close to approaching his standard of play. Just assess what standard you can reasonably hope to achieve and work towards that end. You never know, you might surprise yourself and become a better player than you ever dreamt possible.

If you can play only once or twice a fortnight, it would be unrealistic for you to believe that you could force yourself down to scratch. Settle for the far less demanding target, initially at any rate, of becoming a single figure handicap golfer.

Because of the handicapping system you can play with golfers far better than yourself, and far worse, and have a level game. This, indeed, is one of golf's bonus factors.

BEGINNERS

For anyone taking up the game there is nothing to beat a few hours tuition from a professional – the man whose job it is to help you improve (if you will let him). You can read as many books as you want but nothing compares with the one-to-one relationship of pupil and teacher on the practice ground.

There the professional can watch you hitting shots, spot and correct the faults, and in this respect you may care to go along to one or two professionals in your area to see whose teaching style can best help you. This is not sales talk – it is common sense. Only those with the touch of genius can get by without any help.

It is easy these days to learn about the game and discover whether or not you are going to like it. Most local authorities run golf evening classes during the winter and if you are still at school there is every chance you will have the opportunity to take up the game by courtesy of the excellent Golf Foundation sponsored tuition courses.

If you were to take up tennis I'll guarantee that within a very short time you would be managing to hit the ball over the net. You might even get involved in simple three or four shot rallies but golf is not so quickly mastered.

Assuming you are fit and are not carrying too much excess avoirdupois it needs only a little co-ordination and a keen eye to hit the tennis ball most of the time but you could send someone out 'cold' to play golf and they might take hours to complete the first hole, missing the ball more often than they hit it.

It is essential, therefore, before you step on to that first tee to get the basics – grip, stance, alignment and top of the swing position – correct. You could call them the fundamentals. And I could add another – you really must have equipment that suits your physical capabilities!

One of the great mysteries of golf – and indeed one of its charms – is the realisation that there is no right and wrong way to play, no ideal method which is completely fool proof.

The swing that suits you with your husky build and bulky shape will not suit your next door neighbour if he happens to be 6 feet 5 inches tall and a beanpole into the bargain and the grip which suits you might be totally wrong for him.

What works for Jack Nicklaus does not necessarily work for Severiano Ballesteros, Raymond Floyd, Christy O'Connor or Tony Jacklin. Golf is an individualistic game but while styles vary dramatically the basics remain the same and so too does the objective – to get the ball in 18 holes in as few strokes as possible.

THE GRIP

Your only contact with the club is the grip and if that is wrong, everything could go wrong. If your hands are not operating *together* to control the clubhead throughout the swing but are fighting against each other you will never hit the ball in the direction you want it to go. Golf, in short, will be a misery. There are three grips golfers use: the Vardon grip in which the little finger of the right hand overlaps the first finger of the left; the two-handed or baseball grip in which both hands are firmly on the shaft with no finger overlaps and the inter-locking grip in which the first finger of the left hand and the little finger of the right interlock. Until you have visited a professional you will not know whether you will play best using the Vardon grip, the most popular of the three, the two-handed method which over the years proved highly successful for Welsh Ryder Cup golfer Dai Rees and U.S. P.G.A. champion Bob Rosburg or the interlocking style – a method used by Jack Nicklaus because his fingers were too stubby for him comfortably to use the Vardon grip.

Be prepared to let your professional help you and don't turn down all his suggestions as unworkable without giving them a real try. It is always difficult to change a grip but he might suggest a small adjustment by observing whether or not you have big or small hands, fat fingers or thin and that adjustment might just make all the difference.

Before the Second World War the unkind purists said Alf Perry and the Whitcombe brothers gripped the club the way woodmen grab axes to chop down trees. Bobby Locke, the legendary South African had, in complete contrast, a very weak left hand grip while the late Harry Weetman would spin the club about in his massive hands so much you wondered if he would remember to grab it tightly enough at the right time to hit the ball. He always did of course. Weetman, Perry, the

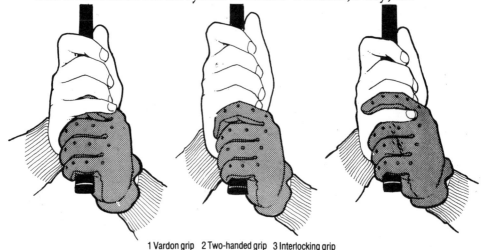

1 Vardon grip   2 Two-handed grip   3 Interlocking grip

Whitcombes and Harry Bradshaw, another with an unorthodox grip, were exceptions to the general rule that success in golf starts with a sound reliable grip. They all had that touch of genius to counteract their idiosyncratic styles. You almost certainly don't – so settle for a proven grip.

There has been much talk over the years about the role of the hands – the left being used to control and guide the club, the right to produce the power in the hitting area but I believe this breakdown produces unnecessary complications and something else to worry about as you go about the business of hitting a shot. Just think of your hands as one unit. Henry Cotton is a great believer in the importance of having good hands – even to the extent of having his pupils hit rubber tyres to strengthen them. Incidentally when Henry talks about 'hitting with the hands' and I talk about hitting with the club head – something you can only do with good hands – or Jack Nicklaus makes references to the vital necessity to have good strong legs we are all talking about the same thing – generating controlled power to hit that ball.

Lay the club across the bottom fingers of the left hand, making sure there are no gaps. Close the fingers to show two to two and a half knuckles when you extend your arm. A good left thumb support on the shaft will help you grip the club more effectively at the top of the backswing. Remember that gaps between fingers and a poor thumb support are the main reasons for loss of control at the top. If that happens you are lost. You will have little hope of regaining control on

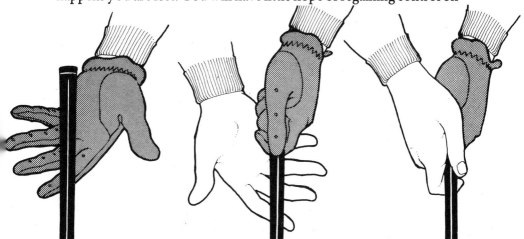

The Vardon grip   1 Start with left hand   2 Overlap right hand   3 'V' is pointing to right shoulder

the way down. Wear a glove on the left hand – especially if you sweat –
as a useful aid to improving that support and consequently control of
the clubhead throughout the swing. Indeed, wear gloves on both hands
if it feels more comfortable.

Now that the left hand is firmly on the club shaft bring in the right
hand so that the little finger hooks over and rests on top of the first
finger of the left hand, helping the hands operate as one – the Vardon
grip is the one we shall concentrate on here. Again the shaft of the club
rests across the bottom of the fingers and the forefinger acts in trigger
fashion, just as it would if it were being asked to fire a gun. Just grip the
shaft comfortably in the fingers with the right thumb going to the left-
hand side of the shaft as you look down the grip. If the thumb is on the
shaft or on the right you will lose power and control. If the back of the
left hand is facing the hole and the back of the right hand is facing away
from it you have it right! In other words the hands are at right angles to
an imaginary line from the target back to the ball and on past it. This is a
big factor in hitting the ball squarely to the target since the hands will
almost certainly return to the square position by instinct. It's like
clapping your hands – you seldom miss!

If your right hand is too much underneath the shaft so that it is facing
more up and down rather than at right angles to the target the grip is too
strong – it's only good for scything grass. This will cause you to
produce a damaging low hook, smother or top because, assuming your
clubface is square, you will be tending to close the face as you

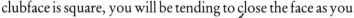

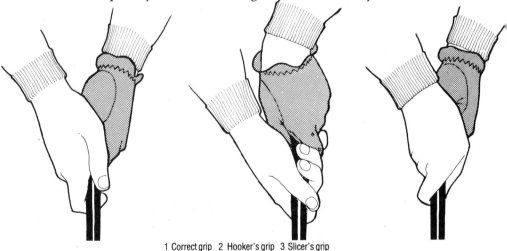

1 Correct grip 2 Hooker's grip 3 Slicer's grip

14

instinctively square those hands up. Similarly, if the hands are tilted in such a way that the back of the right hand is facing up and the back of the left is slightly down your grip is too weak. This time you will pick the club up too sharply and your angle of attack will be way out of line. You will chop at the ball and as a result top it, squirt it along the ground to the right or hit an 110 yard slice! Not good and you have no chance!

THE STANCE

Having got the grip right how should you line up to the ball? How far away from it and how far apart should your feet be?

Make sure, first of all, that your legs are not too stiff or too bent. If you have difficulty in imagining what 'too stiff' or 'too bent' means in a golfing context think of the stance you might adopt if you were about to ski down a gentle slope. Both knees will be relaxed, both legs comfortably stiff and flexed – take care not to have one leg stiff and one bent.

Stand naturally to the ball and if you walk a bit ten to twoish or five to oneish, like me, stand that way when you are lining up. If you try to change things you could find yourself in trouble. Let me explain.

If your left foot is already at ten to two on our imaginary clock on the ground turn your right foot to midday. That will not feel too bad but if you turn your right foot just a little more towards the left so that it is parallel with the left one I can guarantee you are in trouble when you try to swing the club.

You have now adopted an open stance similar to the one used by former Open Champion Lee Trevino, whose genius quotient has helped him make it work. The plain fact is that, for you, turning that right foot in towards the left locks the right hip completely and prevents a smooth turn. You will be thrown off line on the backswing, forced to go outside that imaginary target line and, as a result, will chop across the ball or hit it straight out left as you desperately try to twist and turn to compensate.

Go back to ten to two again and this time move your left foot round to midday and just a little more so that both your feet are almost parallel in the opposite direction. Now your stance is shut. You will find you can take an almighty turn on the backswing because you have no resistance from the right knee or hip – but there is a snag. When you come down to hit the ball you could end up smacking the ground about six inches behind it because you simply cannot get into a position to hit on line for the target.

15

The Stance
1 Alliss ideal – slightly open
2 Wrong – too open
3 Wrong – too closed

A good natural stance is an important brick in the foundation of a solid reliable repeating swing. Your ideal stance should be very slightly open to make it easier for you to turn and then come back to hit the ball away from your body.

You may have been told that as you play through the bag of clubs from driver to wedge the position of the ball in relation to your feet should be moving backwards. It is a theory which over the years has become exaggerated and one with which I don't agree.

As an extreme example, if you had the ball just inside the left heel for your shots with the driver and moved it back an inch or two at a time as you went through the clubs you could find yourself playing your wedge from two or three inches outside your right foot. I doubt it you would hit the ball from that position. If you did you might succeed only in squirting it up your left trouser leg and that could be reasonably painful on a frosty Friday. The early 'move it back' theories were to compensate for the shorter shaft length and the additional loft on the clubs, but if you move the ball back it is the easiest thing in the world to get the left shoulder 'in the way' and become more and more shut to the point at which you are aiming.

I have always favoured having the ball just inside the left heel for all shots (other than a specific shot – into wind, from a bunker or from a sloping lie), then moving further away from the ball and widening the stance as the club shafts get longer.

I often think of my magic triangle as I line up because I find it helps me maintain the ball in the ideal position in relation to both feet whatever type of shot I am playing. This is how it works.

Put a ball down opposite the inside of the left heel. Now move away from the ball with the left foot and move the right foot away from the left, creating the extra width needed for the longer shafted clubs. Line up with a driver, letting the length of the club dictate how far you are from the ball in its position opposite the inside of the left heel.

Now take a shorter iron and move in and forward, still keeping the ball level with the inside of the left heel (most pros do it this way).

16

The Stance
1   Position of ball at address –
    always inside left heel
2   Magic triangle

Maintain a right angle between the ball, the inside of the left heel and the right foot. That right angle of my magic triangle remains constant for every shot.

One advantage of lining up in this way is that your body weight is behind the ball. This will help you sweep away the woods and longer irons. In case you think I am advocating a forward position for the ball, even for chip shots, remember that as you narrow the stance you are effectively 'moving the ball back'. Old books suggested that the width of your stance should never be more than the width of your shoulders, which makes sense – far too many people use far too wide a stance – so be sure not to overdo it. Your feet should be about 18 inches apart from heel to heel for driving, narrowing progressively until you are playing those little chip shots with your feet only three or four inches apart and your knees almost touching.

How far should you stand from the ball? Do not overstretch or stand too cramped. Get the weight onto the balls of the feet. We used to say that if you let the club drop from your hands on to your left leg the top of the shaft would rest just an inch or so above the knee. Do not arch the left wrist upwards or have your hands down between your knees. Looking down, the club should be a natural extension of your relatively straight left arm.

LINING UP

Having considered the grip, the feet and the relationship between the feet and the ball, let us move on to alignment, the set-up that

The Stance 1 Correct 2 Wrong – hands too low, knees not relaxed 3 Wrong – hands too high, knees too bent

is necessary in order to hit the ball towards the chosen target.

I went along once with my father to teach the Cambridge University side. There they were on the practice ground posing at the top of the swing to see if their hands were in the correct position and trying to discover whether or not their right elbow was sticking out or was tucked in.

They had read all the books and knew all about the necessity of keeping the right elbow almost glued to the body as if it was holding a handkerchief in place. They had read about starting the downswing as if they were pulling on the lavatory chain and they knew all about hip rotation and the role of the left heel and so on.

All they were thinking about, in fact, was *from* the ball to the start of the downswing. Few, if any, had stopped for one second to consider cross-checking whether or not they were likely to hit the ball at a target. Yet if you don't know how to aim the ball in the correct direction you will make poor progress as you try to reduce that handicap.

When you play cricket or darts or any game in which you throw an object *towards* something your eye tells you the distance and you throw by instinct. If you are fielding on the boundary and returning the ball to the wicket keeper you don't stop at the top of your backswing to consider if you have taken your arm back far enough, or if you have cocked your wrist at the right time . . . you just throw.

Try to perfect this instinctive action in golf. *Think forward.* I know that sounds rather obvious because hopefully you won't be playing backwards but it is amazing how many amateurs forget to hit the clubhead through and forward. The top pros don't of course.

Your line, as we have said, should be slightly left of the target just as you would line up if you were going to fire a rifle at the pin. When you take aim with a gun you look along the barrel, through the sight and at the target. It is the same principle in golf.

Stand with your shoulders very slightly open and give yourself a chance to hit the ball *away from you* and towards the pin or to the part of the fairway you want to hit. Remember if you have your shoulders, hips and feet *absolutely square* to the target you could be aiming 10–15 yards right of the target, so keep that stance open ever so slightly to stay on line. You will not have got it right if you have to peer over your left shoulder in order to see where you are aiming as you address the ball.

If a line were drawn across your shoulders and hips and across the back of your heels it would run slightly left of the intended line of flight, but remember the club does not always follow the line of the body. If it did you would hook it round you. There is a point when the clubhead is moving away from the body towards the target and the body turning away left.

One final point. Do not listen to those who advocate that you should find out which is your master eye and look at the ball with that. I hope you have two good eyes and would like you to use both. Do not tuck your head into your shoulder like a tortoise or your shoulders will go stiff and will build up tensions. Do not cock your head to one side like a canary in a cage or that dog in the 'His Master's Voice' trademark. Your head may be slightly inclined right because your right hand is below the left on the shaft, your right shoulder below the left but this is natural. *Just don't overdo it.*

Look towards the target then, line up slightly open, keep the knees nicely flexed, the hips relaxed, the head and shoulders loose and grip the club tightly enough to keep control at the top of the backswing. So far so good.

POINTS TO PONDER

Grip the club as firmly as you would hold the steering wheel of your car.

The most important factor in lining up to the target is not the feet but the shoulders.

A SWING THAT LASTS

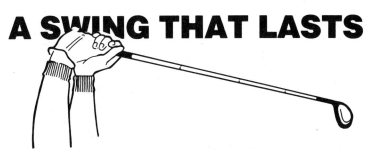

If you have a good grip, a good stance and have lined up properly you are 60 per cent there.

But now we must find that rhythm and fluency that helps us play the game comfortably and more successfully. Some golfers line up with absolutely rigid arms. I am sure you must have seen them on the tee. They look absolutely petrified and needless to say they make a poor attempt at hitting the ball. They may even miss because they lack any kind of rhythm.

I once knew a golfer down at Bournemouth who was a weight lifter in the pre-war Olympics. He was only 5 feet 8 inches tall, but he would lift me up as if I was a featherweight. He could snap golf clubs like toothpicks yet he could never hit a golf ball further than 150 yards because he just could not properly use his power. He had no rhythm, and that's unfortunate.

Harry Vardon once said in answer to someone's comment about his beautifully straight left arm: 'I do not have a straight left arm, but, by George, I do enjoy playing against someone who has.' It was his subtle way of distinguishing between *straight* and *rigid* and you would do well to recognise that difference too.

SWING RHYTHM

Try not to tense up because it is then that you will start making things difficult for yourself and almost impossible to build up any rhythm in the swing.

Do not go to the other extreme, of course, and wobble about on the tee like a jelly on a plate. Your relaxation must be controlled like that of a ballet dancer. Rudolf Nureyev, you know, generates more power in his legs than any golfer ever does but with grace and fluency.

To help you relax take the club out of the bag, swing it backwards and forwards as if you were out walking the dog and were casually clipping off dandelion heads one after the other with a walking stick. Do it naturally. Just let the clubhead swing to and fro and when you come to hit the ball just try to repeat that action.

That may not be as simple as it sounds. How often have we seen splendid practice swings and then when the ball is put down the self-same golfers becoming petrified with fright – their usual reaction being to quit at the point of impact, with devastating results.

The ball does not have any feelings. It does not know whether you are a good golfer or a bad one and responds only to being hit well or badly. There is no need to be mesmerised by it. There is no need to *slow up* and *pull back* as you come into the hitting area in order to, misguidedly, *protect it* in some way or other. The ball has been made to be hit, so do it firmly and with authority.

THE TAKE-AWAY

We are straying from the point, however, the business of building up rhythm, an ingredient you cannot have too much of but something which can be shattered in the first 18 inches of the backswing.

A deliberate smooth, slow opening movement is essential but before you even think of taking the club away cross-check again that you have the fundamentals correct – grip, stance and alignment. A good analogy of the smooth take-away would be letting out the clutch of a car. If you jerk the clutch your car engine will stall and so it is with the golf swing. A quick, jumpy movement at the start is disaster.

Bobby Jones has written that it is almost impossible to swing back too slowly, that sometimes the opening movement can appear to be ridiculously slow but there is no doubt the slower you start back the better you will play because it will help your tempo, it will help you establish a wide arc and will also ensure you go back on the correct line.

Remember, however, there are different degrees of slowness. The take-away of one of those alert bird-like people who lives on his nerves might be slow, for him, but much faster than that of the big pipe-smoking stoic who does everything at a leisurely even pace.

In dealing with the role of the wrists in these first few vital inches of the swing, remember that all the power and precision with which you want to hit the ball is concentrated on the three feet either side of it as you hit it.

All the strength of the backswing is generated simply to take the club back into position from which it will be possible to convert that power into a movement which will help you hit the ball as far as you can within your own capabilities.

Keep the wrists firm for the first 18 inches. If you break the wrists too quickly you will throw your hands out of alignment, force yourself into the wrong position at the top of the swing and be unable to correct the fault on the way down.

Of course it may be argued that some internationally famous golfers have unusual swings and kinks and peculiarities on the way up to the top but they know how to compensate on the way down to bring the clubhead in for a clean hit . . . and you probably don't. My advice is to ignore the professionals in this instance and think instead of ordinary mortals and what they can achieve.

In this first movement of the swing you want to take the clubhead back in a natural way, not forced outside or inside that target line. The take-away will be slightly inside anyway because when you start the movement your right shoulder automatically moves back.

The Take-away 1 Wrong – hands leading the club 2 Wrong – cocking wrists too early 3 Correct

23

Doug Sanders

I might just as well have said that your right hip moves back or have suggested the club comes inside because your left shoulder moves round towards the ball – all are perfectly valid. What is wrong is an opening movement involving the dropping or dipping of that left shoulder! Turn, don't tilt.

Some golfers need something to trigger off the smooth takeway. Gary Player kicks in the right knee while Jack Nicklaus presses very slightly forward with his hands. He also swivels his chin right to allow for the fullest possible turn of the shoulders and in an effort to cut down head movement to the absolute minimum.

If you want to try that head swivel be careful not to dip and throw your shoulders out of alignment and into a closed position. That is always a danger.

TOP OF THE BACKSWING

One important reason for taking the clubhead back initially in one piece is that this will help you turn the hips and shoulders fully. As you coil your body round you are building up power for use later.

Once you break the wrists the object is to *point the club at the target at the top of the backswing* – but this does not mean that you have to overswing.

If you care to think of yourself as having reached the top when your hands are level with the right shoulder then that is perfectly in order. Not completing the backswing properly is one of the main causes of destructive shots, so make sure you get this right. This does not mean, of course, that your backswing needs to be as full as that of Greg Norman. Some professionals with strong hands generating the power can hit a long way with restricted swings. Doug Sanders, the colourful extrovert American who so nearly won the Open Championship in 1970, had a curious half-swing which the jokers said he could use to play out of a telephone kiosk without touching the sides – but he wasn't short off the tee.

As you swing back and your shoulders turn, the legs should move naturally in the same pattern – that is, if you have had them positioned correctly at the start. Resist any temptation to point the left knee towards the target because this will force the weight onto the left and prevent any natural weight transference during the swing. If you turn correctly and don't tilt, the left knee should not create any problems at all.

When I was playing on the tournament circuit, I played all my shots

25

with my left heel *off* the ground at the top of my backswing. I was very long but also very wild, frequently hitting into trouble. Now I keep that left heel firmly *on* the ground and although I may have lost some length I have gained control.

At all times keep the head steady. Think of your body as a windmill with the arms and the club as the sails. Imagine, too, that you have a spindle going right through your body and into the ground, a spindle round which you are going to pivot. The head is like the roof of the windmill. It never moves. If it does your swing will disintegrate.

The most difficult part of controlling the golf swing is getting right the co-ordination of the right to left movement of the trunk with the swing of the arms up, and then down through the ball.

You must try to avoid any excess lateral body movement at this stage. Over the years golfers have talked about the conscious transference of weight from one foot to another but since this is a very difficult thing to learn, I suggest we forget about it all together and concentrate instead on keeping the head still with the arms turning round the body.

Maintain rhythm by thinking of your body as a windmill

26

THE DOWNSWING

Now that you have reached the top of the backswing it is an ideal moment to recap that the only thing which will be hitting the ball is the piece of wood or metal on the end of the shaft.

Don't rush. What we are looking for is power but power with control. Some people to prevent themselves flashing down quickly with their hands believe that they can stop for a fraction of a second at the top but I believe that is a potentially dangerous practice to cultivate and something to be discouraged unless it happens naturally as it does with big Brian Barnes but remember he is an exception. Just be sure you complete the backswing and don't waste clubhead power up at the top when it is that power you are looking for in the hitting area. As the clubhead moves down so your weight will naturally move from the right side to the left and, as the clubhead gains speed, the hands will uncock themselves carrying the club on to a high balanced finish.

HITTING OR SWINGING

People often ask me whether or not they should be trying to hit *down* on the ball at this stage if they are using an iron because they have been told golfers need two swings – one to sweep away the woods, the other for the more lofted iron shots. I have listened to this theory for years and it is all so confusing. In fact you have only one swing although the different loft will make it appear that you have two.

Golfers highlight the suggestion of different hitting techniques by referring to the taking of divots. They have watched tournament stars like Palmer, Nicklaus and Gary Player play iron shots and have seen them sending huge pieces of turf flying through the air. That happens because of the force with which they hit down and through the ball. Beginners would be well advised to ignore the divot taking. In any event Harry Vardon, one of the all-time greats, hardly ever took a divot in his life.

Keep it simple. Use the one swing and the one technique, the same sweeping action, for the majority of your shots.

It is quite clear you will not be able to account for every shot you may have to play in the course of a round. You may not always have a perfect lie – it may be bare or fluffy with the ball lying down but resist the temptation to desert that sweeping action even though you may have to work hard to convince yourself that the clubhead can do the job quite nicely without any additional – and more than likely destructive – help from yourself.

27

Nicklaus in full flow: Like many modern tournament players Jack Nicklaus tends to swing on an upright plain with a very full and wide swing arc. It is a swing which he uses for every club in the bag, except the putter, and which he repeats and repeats even when under the greatest pressure.

Golf is a very complicated game and sometimes even Jack Nicklaus finds shots extremely difficult to play so do not worry if you run into trouble. Just remember you do not help the situation by changing your basic swing.

Remember to get as many things right as early in the piece as you can because you will not have time to think about things when you have started to swing. At best you can remember just one pointer.

Dr Alistair Cochran, who wrote an excellent book a few years ago on the mechanics of the swing, estimated that each shot played took only a fraction of a second and that you spent less than 30 seconds actually hitting the ball during a four hour round.

The margin for error as the club head comes in at 120 miles per hour to hit a ball just 1·68 inches or 1·62 inches in diameter, depending on whether you have an American or British size ball, is very small. Hitting the ball fractionally off centre can mean the difference between hitting the fairway and ending in the rough. Work then on building up a reliable swing but do not expect it to be precision-like right away. You may never achieve the precision you would like in a lifetime of golf. Just keep trying to improve in order that you can get maximum enjoyment from the game.

When Nicklaus is in full flow he becomes that precise windmill we were talking about with his hips rotating and his arms working up and down in perfect co-ordination, repeating and repeating under pressure.

Sometimes, however, things can even go wrong for him. At the U.S. Open at Medinah in Chicago in 1975 he admitted he had resorted to using several swings during the week in order to recover his lost form and the one he plumped for on the final day let him down. He needed three par figures to win or at worst be involved in a playoff but Nicklaus staggered his gallery by dropping shots at the last three holes because of that faulty swing.

If the greatest golfer the world has ever produced can do that sort of thing – albeit infrequently – do not be too disillusioned if you do not go out right away and win the captain's prize. It all takes time.

POINTS TO PONDER

Never tilt or dip that left shoulder when you start the backswing. Turn the shoulder round – not down.

Think of golf as two hands, two arms, two hips and two legs all working as one.

STEPPING ON THE TEE

Many men who play golf are either too proud or too conceited to admit that they might learn more from watching the top women golfers than they ever could watching Arnold Palmer or Johnny Miller.

There are hundreds of amateur golfers who buy the latest Johnny Miller sports shirts, the well-cut Miller slacks to look like the hero in the false hope that by wearing his gear some of his great talent may well rub off on them. Sadly it does not work like that.

There is only one Johnny Miller, only one Arnold Palmer and only one Lee Trevino. You are living in dreamland if you think you will one day match all their achievements – although, of course, there is no harm in trying.

We all enjoy the odd fantasy or two but sadly the fantasy that we are Nicklaus, Tom Watson or Brian Barnes fades quickly when you step on to the first tee. From that point you are on your own and have only your own game on which to rely.

Most amateurs would be far better trying to copy the compact swing and style of some of the top women players such as American Nancy Lopez, the attractive South African Sally Little and the equally decorative Jan Stephenson from Australia, three graceful hitters who earn thousands of dollars each year. One word of warning if you are at a women's event comparing styles – many women do overswing and that is not something to copy.

Like most lady golfers, Sally Little has clubs to suit her punching power, or, if you like, her fighting weight, but here again we are getting back to *getting things right before you start.* Get clubs that suit you!

The classic example of getting equipment tailor-made was the American Doug Ford who had his clubs specifically modelled to take every advantage of his swing deficiencies which were many and varied. It worked. Ford won many tournaments, including the U.S. Masters.

Of course not everyone's swing will match the simplicity of a Tom Watson or a Neil Coles. There always will be golfers with unorthodox

Bill Rodgers

swings like that of Lee Trevino. I often wonder, what would have happened to Trevino if, in the early days, when he was playing for beer money in Mexico someone had taken him aside and tried to 'sort out' his swing . . . stopped him playing all his shots from a point three inches outside his left foot? Would the genius have been an even greater golfer?

Trevino is one of golf's great *manoeuvrers* of a golf ball, a chip shot artist – remember that devastating chip he holed at the seventy-first hole when playing with Tony Jacklin in the 1972 Open at Muirfield which he went on to win. That shot finished Jacklin's hopes and some say Tony has never been the same since. In contrast to Trevino there is the former Open champion, Bill Rogers, whose impressive winning record is built on an uncomplicated swing and marvellous rhythm.

Rogers does not immediately

Far Left: Bill Rogers   Top: Craig Stadler   Left: Jan Stephenson   Right: Johnny Miller

33

give the impression of immense physical power but his sound method enables him to hit the ball at times further than Trevino and often as far as heavyweight Craig Stadler.

PREPARING FOR THE MEDAL

One of the great problems of playing golf is that some people expect to spend a week in the office lifting nothing heavier than a pen or a cup of coffee only to emerge on a Saturday morning on the first tee as a golfing giant.

You know what I mean. The club medal is on, players arrive breathless to drive off, having had no time at all to limber up on the practice range or in the practice net, or even on the putting green.

Curiously these enthusiastic amateurs expect to hit the ball as sweetly as Johnny Miller or Tom Weiskopf when fully warmed up and at their best. It really is most difficult to do that. Nicklaus would never step on to the first tee 'cold' unless in the direst emergency.

If Nicklaus had not played for a week, then made the amateur dash to the tee to be faced with a tight opening drive with an out of bounds to the right or to the left, he would have to concentrate very hard.

If it were really important for him to hit the fairway he would probably take a 3 wood or long iron, grip the club down the shaft for better control and use a lower than normal tee just to make sure of keeping the ball in play.

Yet the handicap amateur with only 10 per cent of Nicklaus' talent whips out his driver and expects to dissect the fairway with a 260 yards drive. If that happened once in twenty times he would be lucky. More often than not the result of such lack of wisdom, of such lack of proper preparedness is a destructive shot, a quickly ruined scorecard and a bad weekend for the family.

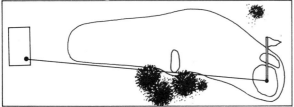

On tight driving holes think twice about using a driver

Give your nervous system a chance. Try to get to the course at least 30 minutes ahead of your starting time in order to have a few practice shots just to break down those adhesions as the well-known teacher John Jacobs always prescribes.

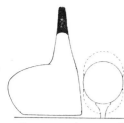

TEEING IT UP

How high do you tee the ball? This is often ignored but it is vitally important. The height should be constant except in extreme weather conditions when you want to flight the ball differently to gain full advantage of the wind.

In general terms, however, the top of the ball should come to just about the top of the clubhead as you address it. Tee it too low and you will have a tendency to fade or even slice; tee it high and it encourages a draw; tee it too high and you risk the danger of coming right underneath the ball, skying the shot and leaving that tell-tale white mark on the top of the club.

NOT ALWAYS THE DRIVER

The driver with its straight face is one of the most difficult clubs in the bag to play so why not switch instead to a 3 wood. That extra bit of loft can not only be helpful, it can also stimulate confidence at the start of the round because you have a better chance of hitting a solid shot.

The Alliss drive

35

Remember Bobby Locke won four British open championships using a driver which had the loft of a 2 wood and Peter Thomson, a five times Open winner, often dispensed with his driver for a 3 wood off the tee when he felt he would get more control and accuracy and when the weather and course conditions permitted. This is thinking man's golf. Before you take out the driver just pause for a moment to ponder whether it is the best club for the job. There is no rule which says you must use it off the tee simply because it is called a driver.

How often when you have been watching top line golf on television or indeed have been following the top players round at tournaments have you spotted famous golfers taking 3 woods and irons off tees at difficult driving holes? The most successful professionals are experts at thinking their way round the course.

WHERE ON THE TEEING GROUND?

Obviously every player wants to hit that ball as far as possible although on dog leg holes this is not always the object. More importantly, however, you will want to ensure you do not send your opening shot crashing on to the railway line, in to the wheat field or anywhere over the course boundary because then you will be faced with the daunting task of hitting a second shot off the same tee but with much less confidence. Accuracy is always more important than length.

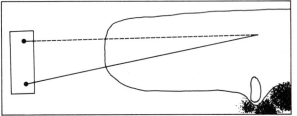

Always tee up your ball close to the trouble

It's amazing how many golfers tee up their ball without considering where the trouble lies for a wayward tee shot. The golden rule is to tee up on the side of the teeing ground closest to the trouble. If there is an out of bounds down the right, like Old Prestwick, tee up *on the right* and hit *your shot out left*. Get as near as you can to the trouble in order to hit the ball away from trouble. This may be psychological but it has helped me over the years and I'm sure it would help you.

The opening drive can be a nerve-racking affair, even more so if you have a target area on the narrow side, lined perhaps by trees or with two fairways bunkers positioned ready to catch the shot not hit absolutely straight.

VISUALISE THE SHOT

What I did in these circumstances was think of my favourite driving hole at Parkstone my old club and flash a picture of it into my subconscious over the top of the real view. Instead of seeing all the trouble before me I imagined a wide open fairway. It worked. I relaxed and consequently I had a better chance of hitting the ball solidly into the narrow gap.

Nicklaus, the most meticulous of golfers, uses a similar visualising technique, only in his case he is thinking purely of the kind of shot he wants to hit. Nicklaus, like many good players, after he has teed up the ball, walks behind it to obtain a visual picture of the shot he wants to hit on that particular hole. The harder he thinks about the shot and its shape and gets it firmly into his subconscious the more chance there is of the muscles helping him reproduce the shot in real life. There is nothing really new in this and if the superstar golfers can fall back on age old practices en route to winning a third million dollars it is well worth slipping them into your routine.

Once Nicklaus has worked out the shape of the shot he selects a spot on the ground some three to four feet in front of the ball and directly on the line the club should take. He concentrates on that point – not the point way down the fairway – to help him hit the ball more accurately where he wants. You might care to try it.

NEVER GIVE UP

If by chance you do hit a poor opening drive and end up with a 7 or an 8 at the hole do not immediately give up, taking the defeatist view that it is just not going to be your day.

Walter Hagen, that great golfing showman between the wars, was in the habit of saying that he expected to hit three or four bad shots in every round and if they all came at the first then he had no more to waste. That's positive thinking and in golf there is certainly no room for despondency if things go wrong. You must only be thinking about your next one, and be more determined than ever to get things right.

Bernard Gallacher did not give up in 1974 in the final round of the Carroll's Irish Open when he began the last round with an 8. He redoubled his efforts and won the £5000 cheque but then that is typical of Gallacher, one of the most determined players on the European circuit.

GET INTO A ROUTINE

Try to condition yourself into believing that you are taking the correct

Lee Trevino:
You cannot legislate for genius!
Trevino is probably the most
unorthodox of the world's
outstanding players. Teeing the
ball in front of his left foot, his
method requires great athleticism
and superb timing.

Advice from the ladies:
Control, rhythm and technique
are more important than
physical strength.

Left: Nancy Lopez (USA)
probably the best-known player
on the American pro-ette
circuit, where she has broken
all sorts of records. Five foot
seven inches tall and strongly
built, Nancy's swing is
characterised by superb
rhythm and her ability to carry
the ball a long way through the
air.

Below: Beth Daniel (USA),
perhaps the most consistent
and exciting player on the
American tour. Five foot ten
inches tall and of slim build,
Beth uses her height to
advantage and her full, flowing
swing allows her to hit far and
straight.

club for every shot you hit during the round and if by chance your opening drive does not go as far as you might have liked do not worry. As you warm up and build up confidence and rhythm so you will begin to hit the ball further with hardly any extra effort. It's maybe an old cliché but do remember that forcing only leads to failure. The slower you swing, the better and the further you will be able to hit the ball.

The no. 1 iron, which like the driver, can be a difficult club to play, can be useful off the tee, the only place on a golf course where you are allowed to tee the ball up. It's a club that the well-built Sandy Lyle often uses very satisfactorily with very little loss of length. Admittedly, many handicap golfers find the 1 iron just a little too tough to play but if you need the accuracy of an iron go down to the 3 which will work almost as well. Have a routine when you step on to the first tee. Breathe deeply and relax. You are going to enjoy it. Swing a couple of clubs to loosen up or do one of the exercises I have often seen Player use – sticking a golf club between the shoulder blades and turning the torso. It all prevents tensing up as you wait for the words 'play away'.

Get those shoulders moving before you step on the tee

POINTS TO PONDER

Give yourself time to warm up before a round. Never play 'cold'. Before you address the ball make a mental picture of the type of shot you want to hit.

FROM THE FAIRWAY

Let us assume that your opening hole is a 380 yards par 4. If you have hit your opening tee shot reasonably straight you will find yourself on the fairway faced with what we normally call an accuracy shot. Whether the shot is 120 yards long or 190 yards long it is the shot with which you are attacking the pin, hopefully to get the ball close enough for a birdie chance.

Study the shot. Look at the pin position. Spot where the main difficulties lie – there could be a stream or two large bunkers or a small hillock, or an out of bounds menacingly close to the putting surface on one side or another. That is the way golf courses are designed. Consider too the ground between the ball and the target. Does it slope towards the pin or away from it? Will the green be fast or slow, depending on whether there has been recent rain? If it is windy how will that affect your shot? All this influences club selection. What you are trying to do is make maximum use of the conditions, take full advantage of the contours of the ground, the wind, if there is any, to get that ball close to the hole. If you do end up hitting a wrongly shaped shot then it is not the end of the world. Learn from your mistake and try not to make the same error in a later game, when faced with a similar problem.

PLAY WITHIN YOURSELF

Remember you will get much more accuracy if you control the *speed of the shot* by taking a club more, a 7 iron rather than an 8, and hitting it firmly but well within yourself than if you try to use the most lofted club you dare and lash at it, losing control in the process. Control is more important than power. It is no use, for instance, taking a wedge from 130 yards out when Nicklaus only uses that club for the 80 to 90 yarders. Be realistic and use an 8 or 9 iron, relying on *feel* and *tempo* to get you accurately to the target. You will be starting to make real progress in golf when you know how to *control the speed of your arms and consequently the clubhead* as you come into the hitting area – but then this is all about tempo, one of the great keys to golf at every level.

41

THAT ELUSIVE TEMPO

Playing much less these days than when I was on the tournament circuit, I have had more time to experiment with tempo. As a result, I feel I have better tempo now than ever before. Of course I was rather frightened to change anything that was working well in the old days. Not so now, and it's fun.

I am now more convinced than ever that the secret of greatness in golf is all tied up with tempo, but I am sorry to say there is no magic wand you can wave to get it or secret formula I can pass on to help you find it. It comes only with hard work and even that cannot guarantee success. Few of us, I am afraid, ever achieve greatness.

If you are on the fairway make best use of that advantage because you could have been unlucky enough to have hit into a fairway trap, to have bounced into the rough or even the heather or landed up behind a tree or small bush. Sometimes, of course, you will land up in a divot mark or in a sidehill, uphill or downhill position on the fairway – but more about these shots later.

THE FADE AND THE DRAW

Sometimes as you look at your target you might like to think of playing an intentional fade or draw to get yourself close to the flag but are you capable of doing this?

You may have been told that to hit a shot intentionally from right to left you strengthen the grip by moving the right hand under the shaft and the left hand over and that you weaken the grip by moving the right hand over and the left hand under for a shot in the opposite direction.

You can influence the shape of the shot purely by altering the position of the hands but really there is far more to it than that. This is one of those occasions where it is better to change the position of the ball and alter the line of attack.

To fade the ball aim left with the ball and the hands forward of the usual position. You can have the ball opposite or even forward of the left toe for the shot with the left foot drawn back – a stance which will help you exaggerate that hit past the chin.

Break the wrists early for a steep take-away and subsequent steep angle of attack then drive the ball forward imparting sidespin as the club head cuts across the ball at impact.

To draw the ball aim right with the ball again forward of the normal position. This time try to imagine that your clubface is a table tennis bat hitting a forehand smash. The clubhead rolls at impact. Try to

Intentional fade: open stance, ball forward, swing outside to in

Intentional draw: closed stance, ball forward, swing inside to out

Greg Norman:
Australia's golf star unleashes a
long iron. Six foot two inches of
bone and muscle, Norman has a
very firm swing arc which keeps
the club on the target line. His
method is simple: take the club
straight back and make it go
straight through.

understand more about those subtle changes in your swing by experimenting on the practice ground. When you are doing this remember to use a medium iron since it is more difficult, because of the added backspin, to fade or draw a lofted iron.

THE IMPORTANCE OF SPIN

Perhaps we should consider for a moment what causes a ball to fly right or left, straight, high or low. The secret is in the spin put on the ball, a spin made more easy by the fact that the golf ball is dimpled – an aerodynamic advantage which the early golfers quickly realised when they discovered their battered gutties flew better later in a round than at the start when they were smooth. If you are the slightest bit technical you will know that no golf ball will fly without backspin to get it in the air. That backspin is created by the loft of the club. The longer, less lofted irons will have a lower trajectory and will not stop so quickly as the shorter ones which have the maximum loft and therefore maximum backspin.

THE LONG IRONS

To many people the playing of long irons, the 1, 2, and 3, is just too difficult. Certainly the small head and the lack of loft can make the clubs look more difficult to play and it is true that you must maintain maximum rhythm on these shots to have any chance of hitting the ball accurately.

Some great golfing professionals have not exactly earned the reputation of being superb long-iron men, so if you are uncertain in this category you are not alone. Golf must be such a positive game that if you do have any doubts do not be afraid to leave the long iron in the bag and plump instead for an easier club: a 4, 5 or even a 6 wood. It's not how you play the shot or what you use that counts, but how many it takes you to hole out. If in doubt always play the shot you are confident you can hit.

THE MIDDLE IRONS

The middle irons, of course, are much easier to play because of the additional loft and the fact that you are approaching the ball from a steeper angle with a narrower stance which helps your control.

Incidentally when you set the clubhead behind the ball at address make sure that the sole is lying flat. If the heel of the club is up in the air, or the toe is, then you will almost certainly fluff the shot. Line up the clubface to target with the bottom of the blade, for this will give the impression of a slightly open position – although it will really be square.

Lining up with the top edge of the blade does tend to make you lay the club in a closed face position. In this instance your eyes actually deceive you, and time and time again when I have pointed out to amateurs that they are hooding the club at address they are genuinely astonished.

Successful golf can be played, of course, when the blade is slightly closed. Neil Coles on the European tour is the best example of a great player whose style is to shut the clubface at address. It only proves again that there is no best way to play the game!

Sometimes you may wish to punch in an iron shot low under the wind. In this situation take a less lofted club than you would normally, shorten your grip down the shaft, put your weight 60 per cent on the left foot and your hands forward. This time your wrists will break earlier, the swing will be steeper and the ball will fly on a low boring trajectory. In windy Britain you may find yourself playing this type of iron shot far more often than you might imagine, especially if you play by the seaside.

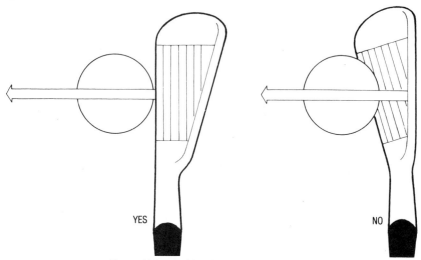

YES   NO

Line up with the sole of the club, not the top of the club face

KNOW THE DISTANCE

Perhaps you think that yardage charts and all that paraphernalia are just for the tournament professionals travelling round the world playing a different course every week but, you know, yardage information could prove useful to you at your home course.

You would need to know how far you hit each club but that is easily

Neil Coles

enough done. If the club does not have an adequate practice ground find an open space somewhere and set up your own targets. Pace out the 50, the 100, the 150 and the 200-yard marks and spot them with a sweater, a golf bag, a pair of waterproof trousers – anything.

From this rough measurement guide you will be able to assess how far you hit each club on average – that is important – not when you hit one of your Sunday best shots which happen only once in a while.

Most amateur golfers rely on sight for their club selection but this can be misleading. How often have you seen players in two minds, changing and replacing clubs? A yardage chart backed up by your own club and distance guide can help you select clubs more accurately, play more authoritatively and trim shots off your score.

PLAY THE PERCENTAGES

If you are unlucky enough to find your ball in one of the more awkward spots on the fairway with the ball lying down in a patch of thickish grass or on the side of a small bank the first thing to remember is not to be too ambitious. It may well be far more prudent to sacrifice distance in favour of accuracy and to rely on a pitch and putt for your par, rather than put your faith in a difficult-to-play shot which could get you to the green if you hit it flush but which will not if more than likely you don't.

Think of those percentages again. Weigh up what you stand to gain with what you could lose. Ask yourself whether or not it is worth dropping a shot, or even two, just to take a foolhardy swipe at the ball.

SLOPING LIES

Learn to play shots from sloping lies so that when you are faced with them you know what you are trying to do. Golf from a level stance is difficult enough. It becomes more difficult if the ball is on a slope. You have nothing to fear, however, if you are selective in your club choice and know how to adjust your method.

Let us suppose you have hit your ball on to a slightly downhill lie – I don't mean a precipice, just the kind of slope you might find yourself on if you were playing over the Old Course at St Andrews or at Royal St George's where it is sometimes difficult to find a reasonably large flat area of turf.

If you think you can reach the green with a 4 iron, take a 5 iron. Why? Because of the slope of the ground, the ball will fly further and lower from this kind of lie. By going down a club you are compensating for the conditions. Aim slightly right – the right half of the green if the pin is centrally positioned, to counteract a tendency to hook.

48

For an uphill shot you will have to take one or even two clubs more than you would normally since the ball will fly higher and consequently less far than off a flat lie. The tendency of the uphill lie will be to draw the ball so once again aim right of target, open the club face to counteract any club head roll on impact and resist that temptation to hit the ball really hard.

With both these shots there should be as little body movement as possible and to this end I advocate leaning into the shots ever so slightly so that you can retain your balance.

Very little footwork is required in these situations and it is important to stick to your normal, easy swing, following through so that the clubhead follows the contours of the slope.

If the ball is above your feet as you play it you will again have a

Left: downhill lie use one club less Right: uphill lie use one club more

Tom Weiskopf:
Standing six foot three inches tall,
Weiskopf can send the ball
enormous distances yet, like
many of the top stars, he tries
most of the time to play within
himself.

tendency to hook so make allowances by aiming slightly right and opening that clubface just a little. Swing through slowly but firmly and in order to maintain your balance on the sloping fairway dig in with your toes, shorten the grip and use a three quarter swing.

If the ball is below your feet it must be further away than it would be off a normal flat lie. As you play it grip the club at the end, bend your knees to retain balance and on no account *overswing* because then you will run the risk of shanking the shot, (that is, hitting it off the neck of the club) or missing it altogether. A good analogy for what you are trying to do comes from motor racing. It is easy to drive a racing car at 125 miles per hour down a straight by putting your foot hard down on the accelerator but you are in dire trouble when you come to the sharp bend at the end.

Left: standing below ball, aim right, open club face slightly Right: standing above ball, aim left, close club face slightly

So it is with the shot in which the ball is below your feet. Work out how hard you can hit and sweep the ball away without losing control and missing it. Off this kind of lie the ball will tend to fade or even slice, so make allowances by closing the clubface slightly and aiming to the left of the green.

It will be worth your while to practice those sloping shots under the trained eye of the club professional. He will help you learn how to hit them with finesse and confidence.

Few fairways in this country are completely flat so you will be faced regularly with this kind of shot. If you remember at all times to maintain your rhythm and to stay down on the shot well into the follow-through area you should have no fear in sloping lie situations.

Weight evenly balanced perhaps favouring left foot, ball positioned right of centre, head steady

Head still steady and swing back normally

Swing through normally and because the club arc is following the slope your follow through will be curtailed

POINTS TO PONDER

Always play within yourself. Overclubbing is rarely a fault for handicap golfers.

Maintain an even tempo and stop swinging fast by counting yourself through the swing. One-and-two with the 'and' that crucial change of direction at the top.

AROUND THE GREEN

For shots to the green from much shorter range it is more important than ever to hit the ball with the clubhead moving through in a nice easy smooth action.

Try whenever possible to land the ball on the green every time from at least 30 yards out unless, of course, you are playing on one of those hard, fast seaside links with no greenside fringe where it might be more prudent to run the ball up to the hole perhaps even with a putter.

Chipping on to the green is rather like playing bowls. If you were to stand on the edge of the green with two or three golf balls and were to 'bowl' them one by one towards the pin it is more likely that your first attempt would finish way beyond, or well short. Having taken into consideration the texture of the grass and the contours of the green you will quickly become expert at lobbing the ball close to the hole.

The ball is *round* and I cannot stress too strongly that when it lands on the green it will *roll.*

Seldom in Britain will you see balls spinning *back* in the way they do in those telecasts of the U.S. Masters or the U.S. Open. Remember a ball will spin back *only* if it lands on a *receptive green,* one that has been heavily watered.

I love the story about Henry Cotton who was supposed to have played a 2 iron shot downwind to a green sloping away from him at St Andrews. The ball apparently bounced, then checked and stopped. I would have loved to have seen it. Those who did must have had a real treat but I wonder if it landed on a damp patch or if it is like so many other golfing stories that improve with age.

PITCHING

Before we go any further let us make sure we know the difference between the chip shot and the pitch.

A pitch involves maximum carry and minimum run, the kind of shot you would play to get the ball up and over a bunker or stream from as far out as 90 yards.

A chip involves minimum air flight and maximum roll, the type of shot you could play if there was little trouble between you and the pin.

When pitching the ball you are doing in miniature what you did with the full shots except that you may be using a half to three-quarter swing, depending on the distance. The further the shot the greater the swing. There is no need to worry about hitting down at this stage because you will steepen the angle of attack by moving closer to the ball when you narrow the stance. The pitching wedge, in particular, is designed to live up to its name. As long as you hit the ball crisply, and avoid 'scooping' with your hands, the club will do the rest – the ball will fly high, bounce

once or twice on the green and stop. If you get the opportunity try to watch a short-game expert like Bernard Gallacher playing this shot.

Bernard Gallacher pitching with a bunker between him and the flag

CHIPPING

For little chip shots do not grip the club too tightly or swing too sharply. Give yourself *room to swing*. Use an open stance – that is, one with the left foot drawn slightly back from the line of flight. Do not break the wrists at all – just take the hands back to hip height and follow through with a nice easy rhythm so that you take the sting out of the shot when it lands on the green, but still allow it to *roll forward* to the hole.

In the early days I used a 4 iron for those little chip and run shots as did many of the old-time professionals but now I use a 7 iron when I want to run the ball a long way, and a 9 iron when the pin is nearer and there is only six to ten yards with which to work. I always try to obtain a mental picture of this shot. I visually select a spot between me and the flag on which I want the ball to land, then play the shot firmly and with

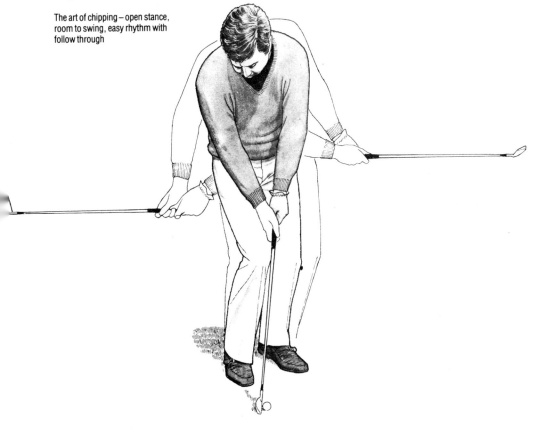

The art of chipping – open stance, room to swing, easy rhythm with follow through

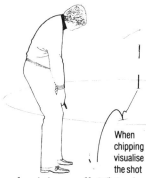

When chipping visualise the shot

my head rock steady – very important. If my mental picture has been correct and my feel for distance accurate then the result ought to be satisfying with the ball finishing within four feet or so of the hole.

If the pin is really in close I use a pitching wedge or even a sand iron for those delicate little shots for which I will be opening the face and cutting the ball up to make it hang in the air, then fall limply on to the green with no elasticity at all. This shot really does demand maximum control. Never jerk this shot and do not try to flick at the ball. Swing easy and slow.

PRACTICE MAKES PERFECT

For chipping and close range pitching get to know how to use your clubs in subtle ways by opening or shutting the clubface by moving the hands up and down the shaft or getting them in front of the ball.

It is the type of practising you can do in your garden. Neil Coles, one of the most beautiful chippers in golf, does it for hours on end when he is at home. His target areas are the rockery, a hammock and a deck chair but it could just as easily be a bucket or a wheelbarrow or an empty cold frame in your garden.

How many shots, I wonder, do you drop in a round because you lack the confidence to play to the pin? How many times have you reached into your bag for your putter from 20 yards out when you know that you should really be taking a lofted club. A putter will only give you a safety shot from off the green when the grass is dry and short. Chipping is perhaps the part of the game that leaves room for most artistry. It's got nothing to do with power but with judgment and instinct. There is nothing quite so valuable as the knowledge you receive in acquiring the feel of a ball *going off the clubhead at the right speed* – and that can only come from practice.

BUNKERS

Sometimes your approach from mid-fairway will roll into a bunker. There is a marvellous mystique in the minds of many players that bunkers are impossible to get out of. They are difficult but not impossible.

Yet I know how frustrating it is to be told regularly that it is easy to recover from a bunker when you are not too proficient at it and can take two or three shots each time to 'escape'.

Basically there is not a professional golfer who cannot get out of a greenside trap first time if asked to do so, assuming the ball is not plugged in the bank or buried in soft sand.

Yet the handicap golfer usually counts himself lucky to get the ball out never mind on to the green. The reason is simple enough to understand. Most amateurs swing at the ball instead of *down and through it*. They want, of course, to get the shot over as quickly as possible and they fail to concentrate.

SAND WEDGES

Sometimes they are not helped to play the proper shot because of the club they are using. Try to make sure you have a sand wedge in your bag that is suited to the bunkers at your home course – the course where you probably play at least 90 per cent of your golf.

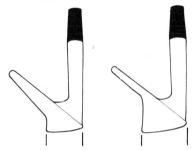

Left: narrow flange for heavy course
Right: wide flange for sandy course

If you play on a heavy course with hard muddy bunkers then you will need a sand club with a sharpish leading edge to allow you to cut the ball out rather than blast it clear.

If you play at a seaside course with those cavernous bunkers filled with foot after foot of soft white sand into which you feel you are going to sink, you will need a club with a wider flange that does not bury deeply at impact, preventing any kind of follow through.

Those seaside bunkers are much the most awkward from which to recover. Not only is it sometimes difficult to get a firm stance in the sand, there is also every likelihood that the ball will be completely buried. Then it is just a hope-and-hit shot.

THINK FORWARD

The basic mistake most golfers make is that they try to flick the ball out and that simply does not work. Do not hurl the body at the ball. Swing the head of the club just as you did for the little rhythmical pitch only this time harder. Grip the club in the normal way, well up towards the end of the shaft for you will make it almost impossible to swing fully if you grip it close to the bare shaft.

Keep the hands together, just like you did for the chip shots, keep the legs relaxed and maintain a smooth pendulum-like swing with almost no wrist action at all. Never spoon the ball out with almost no backswing and a terrific follow through. You will almost certainly fail.

The ideal bunker shot – hands together, legs relaxed, smooth swing

58

What really throws the ball out of the bunker is the shock of sand piling up on the clubface as you hit *down and through*. That is why it is vitally important to keep the *club going forward*.

You would be surprised at how many people dig the clubhead into

Left: the flicker who usually thins the ball across the green or into the face of the bunker

Right: the quitter who forgets to follow through and usually leaves the ball in the sand

the sand and leave it there, forgetting to follow through. They are surprised when the ball remains in the trap but these poor souls are the 'quitters' of golf . . . the golfers who forget to think 'forward'. Tommy Horton, although not a big man, has strong hands and arms and can really control the clubface in these conditions. He never blasts out. Hitting about an inch behind the ball, he uses the weight of the clubhead to do the job, 'shocking' the ball out on a thin layer of sand. The professionals are really worth watching in sand, look particularly at how they keep the clubhead moving *through the ball.*

Gary Player has over the years built up quite a reputation as a bunker player but, marvellous though he is, I don't think he is any better than say Australian Norman Von Nida, our own Dai Rees, Chi Chi Rodriguez, Sam Snead or Julius Boros at their peak. Player's great ability in bunkers is coupled with the equally great talent of being able to hole out relentlessly from four, six and eight feet for his par.

Tommy Horton demonstrates his bunker technique

Gary Player

THE BURIED BALL

If the ball is really buried in the sand then I use a Chi Chi Rodriguez method of getting it out – a method he demonstrated when we played together a few years ago.

I had always believed that the way to dislodge a ball that was buried was to dispense with the sand iron, take a 9 iron with a sharper flange, shut the face and smash into the sand two inches or three inches behind the ball. With any luck it would come shooting out.

I became quite good at the shot, the stunning shot, played with the head of the club slightly hooded but there was one big disadvantage. Because I took so much sand this reduced the backspin and consequently when the ball landed on the green it ran and ran and ran out of control.

Then came Chi Chi's revelation. I changed my style completely. What he did was take a sand iron and *open the face.* Then he put his hands ahead of the ball, took an open stance and on the backswing *broke* the wrists very quickly for an upright take-away. As he hit into the sand he imagined the clubhead *not* going down and through, up and out, but rather going *down and down into the trap* as if trying to bury the clubhead in the sand a few inches beyond the ball with hardly any follow through. It worked for me. I found it to be a great help for this specific shot.

Playing a normal bunker shot

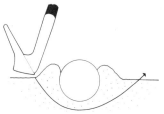

Playing a buried ball bunker shot

WEIGH UP THE OPTIONS

If your ball is lying in the front section on a rather steep uphill part of the trap, you must hit the sand nearer to the ball because you will initially be going through deeper sand than normal. This will tend to slow up the clubhead. If the ball is on a downhill slope aim to hit the sand further behind the ball than normal. In both cases keep that club face open.

In learning and appreciating what you are trying to do when you step into a bunker remember to study the shot. If the bunker is flat and the sand baked hard you have the option of playing a 7 or 8 iron. If the

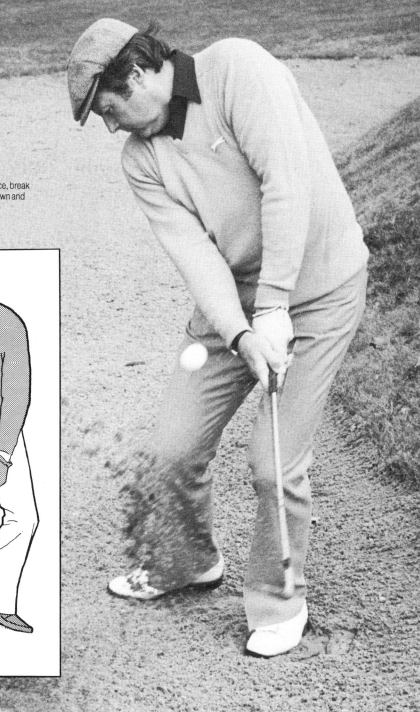

Buried ball – open club face, break wrists early, hit steeply down and follow through

bunker has no lip you might be able to putt it out, remembering, of course, never to let the club touch the sand or you will be penalised. It is terribly important if you do use a putter to make solid contact, and hit the ball firmly.

Probably the most difficult bunker shots to play are those from 30 to 50 yards out because it is always difficult to judge the distance and to know how much sand to take. If I have to get the ball up and out of a trap and then carry it some 50 yards to the stick I imagine the bunker has a steep face over which I have to get to the green.

By concentrating hard on getting the ball up and over my imaginary bank I usually hit the green comfortably enough and sometimes may even have got near enough to the pin to give myself a birdie chance. It has often been said that golf is a tremendous character builder, and never more so than when the ball is bunkered. When you step into that trap, you must believe in yourself and your method. It really is a test of the mind. Remember to swing *slowly, smoothly and follow through*. Do this and I think you will find that bunkers will very quickly lose that 'mission impossible' tag. One final point, time enough to think about getting near the flag once you have started to get out regularly first time.

POINTS TO PONDER

The key to a successful swing is a firmly positioned head. Keep it still throughout the swing.

Never rush your swing in a bunker. Swing slowly and deliberately, with a good follow-through.

PUTTING

It is often said that the game of golf is two games – the art of getting the ball on the green and the skill of holing out.

If we analyse the game at close quarters it could be argued that driving, where you are allowed to put the ball on a tee, and putting where you are playing across a specially prepared surface must be the easiest parts of the game but that would be so wrong. Just think of the anguish golfers have faced over the years on the green because of poor putting.

Unfortunately, whether you care to admit it or not, putting has become 80 per cent of the modern game of golf. A century ago, when those old Scottish worthies Tom Morris and Willie Park were playing their golf at St Andrews and Musselburgh, their winning skill was the skill of getting on to the green in as few strokes as possible, but now it is all so different.

Today many people feel putting plays too important a part in major tournaments and championships. All too frequently, say the critics, it is the golfer who putts best rather than the one with all round excellence who takes the top prize, which can sometimes amount to as much as 100,000 dollars.

This is certainly the case in America where the courses are tailored to give a maximum reward for a good drive and where the approach shots are nearly always fired into well-watered receptive greens.

When the greens are prepared in a different way to normal (as the U.S. Open each year) and the players face up to putting surfaces as smooth as marble table tops some of them waste no time in voicing their complaints to anyone who will listen.

No one can argue that there is a 'best' method for putting since putting is basically feel, intuition and inspiration – 98 per cent inspiration according to Jack Nicklaus. The best method for you is the method with which you can more often than not hole out . . . assuming, of course, that method does not contravene any golf rule.

The rules do not allow you to straddle the line of the putt with your legs and putt croquet style into the hole since this is considered to contravene the traditional idea of a golf stroke.

There are some professionals on the European tour who will never be great putters as opposed to good ones because they appear to lack the necessary sensitivity on the greens. There are a few younger golfers whose progress is slower than might have been expected because, while their long game is good, their putting is suspect.

THE POWER OF POSITIVE THINKING

What every player can do, whether or not he has the bonus of sensitivity or not, is to give himself every chance to hole out successfully by assessing accurately the speed of the putt, deciding positively the line of the putt (and sticking to that decision) and thinking at all times in a positive manner.

If you think that you are going to miss the putt that will give you a much needed birdie or will save your par then more often than not you will. If you honestly believe you can hole it you will be surprised how often it does go in. When I was on the tour a few years ago I played with golfers who willed the ball into the hole, their attitude was so positive. It dared not miss! A good tip for handicap golfers is to watch the juniors at their club putting. Youngsters expect to hole everything and watch the look of surprise on their faces if they do miss a ten-footer.

To adopt such a positive approach you must be confident you have

The Nicklaus putting method. Consider the putt, hit the ball firmly. In she goes!

66

the direction and speed correct when you hit the ball and that you are using a putter with which you are happy.

WHAT KIND OF PUTTER?

If there is one club in the bag that is associated with faith, superstition, perhaps even witchcraft, it is the putter. It is a subject on which it is difficult to give advice but here goes. If your course has heavy greens or greens on which the grass is thick and hardly ever shaved down then you need a fairly heavy-headed club if only to help you hit the ball up to the hole.

If you play down by the seaside where the greens are likely to be slick and fast, where the grass is reasonably fine and the lines more subtle you will need a lighter putter. This is a general rule of course, but like most things in golf, it does not always hold good. End of lesson! What you are really looking for is the putter you feel happiest with when you are on the course, a putter which has a nice balance, and a sweet spot on the clubhead which suits your style.

Putters come in all shapes and sizes but when selecting one for yourself, take into consideration the balance and the feel of the club, check on its weight and the length of the shaft.

Your build will also be a most important factor in deciding the style of putter you use. If you are small and stocky then you will find it difficult to use an upright putter with a vertical lie. You will probably be better off with one that is much flatter. The opposite is usually true for the tall and lean player.

Some players stick to the same putter most of their lives. Jack Nicklaus used his trusty blade putter through the '60s and '70s because it felt right and he usually putted well with it. Perhaps he is now losing confidence in it because he has been experimenting with other models over the past two seasons. Another record-breaking golfer who stuck by his putter, 'Calamity Jane', through thick and thin, was Bobby Jones. During my professional career on the other hand I used something like forty putters, thinking I had found the right one every time and discovering a couple of tournaments later that I was wrong. Frequently you will hear of players who experiment with this putter or that for a time only to return eventually to the putter which won them a major tournament – maybe in the hope that the old magic is still there. It would be nice to think that, somehow, a putter did most of the work on the green by itself but being realistic, of course, the putter can only do what the person holding it makes it do. When the golfers complain that their putter let them down what they really mean is that their ability to judge line and pace has let them down or the second shots were so far from the hole this let them down!

FAMOUS AND NOT SO FAMOUS PUTTERS

That old hickory-shafted putter that Uncle Bert left you in the bag of old clubs he used before the war might well have worked for him but you would improve your putting 100 per cent if you tried a modern club. There is no room for sentiment in golf (even when it comes to putters) but while I urge you, initially, to experiment do not discard the old club simply because it is old. Bobby Locke used a hickory-shafted club for most of his illustrious golf career and was so good that he made 'headlines' when he missed from three feet on one occasion!

Illustrating the fact that the club that suits you is the one you hole the putts with I remember in 1948 when Norman Von Nida, the wiry little Australian, won the Dunlop Masters at Sunningdale. He did so using a putter he bought from a member of the club on the putting green during the event. Von Nida had paused to watch an old member putting away on the practice green with an old George Nicoll blade putter. As he was practising a fellow member of the club strolled along and produced from his pencil-slim bag a Braid-Mills aluminium headed putter, one of those clubs with a head shaped like a letter D. As Von Nida watched in fascination, both old timers holed out with a monotonous regularity. Needless to say, negotiations took place and Von Nida bought both clubs. He paid £50 for one and gave away a set of Tommy Armour Silver Scot woods for the other. Then with the hickory-shafted blade putter he went on to fire a final round of 63 to win the tournament. Afterwards someone was discussing why he had paid such a sum of money – £50 was worth a lot in those days – for a putter, but Von Nida had a straightforward enough answer. 'I'd pay £50 every week for a putter if I knew I was going to hole putts regularly enough to win a £400 first prize each time.' That put everything into perspective . . . yet for all I know he may never have used either putter ever again.

Of all the professionals I played with during my career no one had a more bizarre collection of putters than that man of real genius, Max Faulkner. He did not, of course, limit his eccentricity to putters – he had thin-bladed pitching wedges, drivers which were inches longer in the shaft then normal, irons with ram-rod shafts and others with shafts which were so whippy they were like those rubber ones the late Paul Hahn used in his highly entertaining trick shot act.

68

Tom Watson

As for putters I remember on one occasion Max was using a club made out of an old piece of driftwood he had picked up on the beach. The home-made putter worked for him that week just as any modern club would have. I often wondered had the irrepressible Max played his tournament golf with a properly matched set of clubs would his record have been all the more impressive? I doubt it. Max, with his extrovert personality, bizarre clubs, colourful dress sense and sometimes way-out opinions, never found it difficult to make headlines but, of course, he also had a superb golf game.

I remember my father telling me always to beware of the man who turns up with a brand new set of clubs and an awful looking putter. I had scoffed one day at the tattiness of a putter in an otherwise impressive bag of clubs a visitor was using at Parkstone. The putter had a narrow wooden head, very shallow at the front and scooped out. The grip was held together by bits of string and the shaft was ludicrously whippy. 'Beware', said my dad, sensing my mocking tone, 'a man who has a club like that in his bag would not be such a bloody fool as to have it if he did not play well with it. You can be sure he knows how to use it.' That man went on that day to win the competition!

It is a strange thing about putters that when you pick up someone else's club it almost *swings by itself* in the way the famous owner uses it. It's as if it could not work in any other way. Or am I getting carried away by my own superstitions? Anyway, I am sure if you picked up Bobby Locke's putter you would feel obliged to *try and putt the way he does* with a closed stance, drawing the ball towards the hole. Similarly with U.S. star Hubert Green who adopts a particularly wide stance, his weight forward on his left leg and his hands well in front of the ball. Pick up his putter and you would find yourself almost involuntarily adopting his crouching style and stance. And how well it works for him!

PUTTING GRIPS AND STYLES

Many golfers change their grip for putting. Nicklaus uses an interlocking method for his shots through the green but changes to a reverse overlap for putting. Johnny Miller changes from a Vardon grip to the reverse one because he says it ensures that all four fingers of the right hand – the sensitive fingers of the putting stroke – are on the club shaft.

Both these men 'reverse' – that is, they lay the forefinger of the left hand over the fingers of the right hand – very successfully, and you might want to experiment.

There are so many different ways to putt that it is pointless to recommend this way or that in preference to a third or any other method. There are as many styles as there are stars in the sky. Gary Player, uses a hunched up crouching style with his elbows tucked right into his body and his wrists high. He gives the ball a sharp rap, while Lee Trevino, in keeping with a long game style that is very personal, uses a putting technique that is very wristy and flowing. Billy Casper, who over the years built up a reputation as one of the world's great putters, uses an arm and wrists method but Bob Charles, the New Zealand left hander, favours the arms and shoulders technique. He is one of the golf's most successful long range approach putters and has been unbelievably successful with his firm wristed pendulum style. Then, of course, there is Sam Snead doing the next best thing to croquet style, within the rules, just to keep sane on the putting green. Like some older golfers he had to find an answer to the 'yips' and so he devised a special style. He stands parallel to the line of the putt facing the hole using the putter in what is described as *side-saddle* fashion with the right hand well down the shaft on a special grip down by the blade. It certainly works for him and dramatically reduced his tournament average from forty-two to thirty-three putts a round.

Reverse overlap grip

HIT THE BALL SQUARELY

Charles takes the club back with the left hand and putts with his right. Nicklaus takes it back with his right and putts with the right but I think all this confuses and complicates. I go back to the original premise that golf is two-handed and separating the roles of each hand adds unnecessarily anxious thoughts at a time when the mind should be clear to think only of holing out.

Take the putter back in the most comfortable way, keeping in mind that you must get that blade square to the ball for the strike. Keep your hands just level with the ball at the set up just as you do for all the shots or if it feels more comfortable just marginally in front.

71

Keep the wrists firm.

At the 1977 Open Championship at Turnberry Mark Hayes, the young American, smashed a 43-year-old Open record when he went round in 63 – and he putted left-hand-below-right. Hayes' crosshanded or cackhanded method worked so successfully for him on that day that even Arnold Palmer tried it for a time. Cackhanded putting has long been thought of as a stop-gap method for someone who has lost his or her putting nerve, but quite a few golfers do use this method all the time in America, notably Bruce Leitzke who is a multiple winner.

Isao Aoki

Bruce Leitzke

When Nicklaus putts he lines up and aims on a spot a few inches in front of the ball on his chosen line, just as he does with his woods and irons. Johnny Miller, on the other hand, likes to visualise the whole line of the putt. I favour the Nicklaus style of choosing a spot over which to aim. I take the view that once you have studied the line carefully, from every angle if need be, and decided on the strength of hit, every putt becomes a *straight putt*. It simplifies to think of putts this way, erasing the borrow from your mind after you have decided on the line. Think of pace, think positively, and give it a run.

Many putts are missed because golfers have not been prepared to decide on a line, then hit the ball along it. They cannot make themselves accept a three-inch or nine-inch borrow or face up to the fact that the clubhead hitting the ball firmly along the chosen line can do the job very

Hubert Green

satisfactorily. They try to help the ball along the route, turning their hands on it and closing the clubhead or opening it and distorting the chosen path. In other words, they push out a left to right putt and often hook one in the other direction. Once you have made up your mind about the borrow, live with it. Hit the putt firmly along it and forget about any last minute compensations. And that tip is particularly important on sloping greens. Whether the borrow is left to right, or vice versa, choose a spot over which the ball is going to run and aim for it. Remember that if your ball is above the hole as it approaches it can still fall in, if it is below it you have missed as soon as the ball leaves the putter. In other words, if you chicken out on the borrow you will miss 'on the amateur side'.

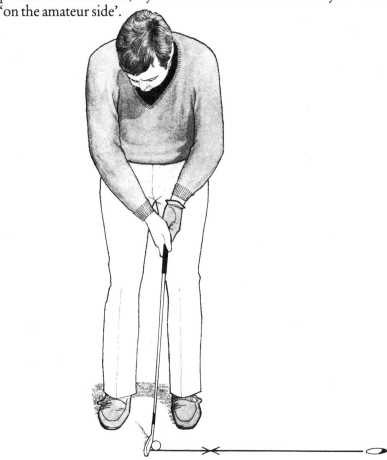

Select an aiming spot between the ball and the hole

HEAD OVER THE BALL

When you are lining up make sure that your eyes are above the ball or if they are in front or behind it that they are on a line which, if extended through the ball towards the hole or back from it, would be the line you plan to take to the hole. If you are too far over the ball and your eyes are beyond the ball as it lies on the green waiting to be hit you will almost certainly miss on the right. If you are not far enough over you will miss on the left because your eyes will mislead you into taking a different line to the one you have really chosen.

You may be a bold putter like Arnold Palmer – how often have you admired the way he charged the ball in when he was at his peak and, if he

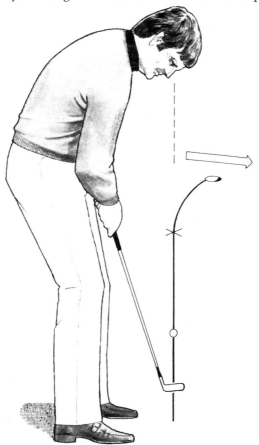

Making your mind up about borrow, select aiming spot, head over ball, hit putt firmly.

missed, the confident manner he holed those three or four footers back
– or you might prefer to use the 'die-at-the-hole' method favoured by
Jack Nicklaus, but face up to the fact that you will not necessarily putt
well every week. You are just as likely to putt well in hot streaks like
Tony Jacklin and you will not be able to pinpoint exactly why.

TEMPO ON THE GREEN

Since putting is a question of feel more than anything else – 75 per cent
feel, 25 per cent method – it is logical that some days you will be better
than others . . . but you can always be sure of controlling one thing –
the strength with which you hit the ball. That can be practised. Just as
rhythm is important on your shots to the green so it is on the green.
Nothing can beat a smooth, even tempo whether you favour a long
backswing and a short follow through, like Peter Thomson, or whether
you adopt Johnny Miller's method of consistent length of backswing
but varying the length of the follow through according to the length of
the putt.

I prefer the Miller style with its standard backswing length but I .
know that Nicklaus does the opposite, extending the backswing if he
wants to hit the ball harder. It is a matter of choice . . . but whatever
you use keep the rhythm going all the time and do not stop or slow
down when you come to the ball.

You should work hard at becoming a good judge of hitting the ball at
the right speed, getting to know the feel on the clubhead.

Give yourself every chance to get the speed correct by taking into
account whether the grass is heavy or fine, wet or dry and whether the
putt is into or down the grain, that is, with or against the blade of grass. I
am amazed sometimes at the way golfers throw away strokes because
they fail to do this simple preparatory exercise. You know what I mean.
Because they have had to hit the ball quite hard up to the hole on the first
two greens they do it automatically on the third without apparently
realising that that green has just been cut. When the ball scuttles eight or
even ten feet past the pin they seem surprised, shocked and let down.
They did not take enough care.

The closer you can get on these longer putts the less likely you will be
to miss those nasty three footers – the putts that psychologically most of
us fear because we know we should not miss them but frequently and
agonisingly do. Some golfers, to help cope with the agony of these yard
and less putts, have tried all sorts of dodges to avoid an embarrassing
miss. They have widened their stance so that their left foot is almost up

to the hole or they have closed one eye (or even both!) and listened instead for the sound of the ball hopefully dropping into the cup. The danger of playing it 'blind' is that you might miss the ball altogether. Make a serious effort to keep your head down during the stroke, resist the temptation to look up to catch a glimpse of your glory putt because if you do, you will miss out on the glory as you pull your body off line. It is probably not much consolation but do remember that everyone is going to miss a short putt sometime – even a nine-inch putt if they hit it in anger or are just plain careless. The important thing to do is to forget it, erase it from your mind before you play your next tee shot or it is liable to be a destructive influence. You have made your mistake, now concentrate on your next shot.

PRACTICE PUTTING

It is important to get the sound of the ball falling into the cup firmly imprinted in your mind because it helps to convey a positive attitude. I know of professional golfers who have spent two hours on the practice green just putting into the cup to remind their subconscious of how it sounds in order to give themselves a psychological boost before they

Tom Kite on the practice green

Bob Charles

play their next round . . . and it seems to work. Usually they do putt better even if marginally so afterwards. Spend your time on the practice putting green perfecting your putting stroke and your positive attitude by holing out from various ranges and from various angles. It is of little use putting over and over again from the same spot into the hole after you have decided the line . . . and found it to be the right one. Do what some tour golfers do. Select a hole and then work in clockwise fashion round it holing out from every angle.

Bob Charles did not become a great putter overnight. He had to practise hard and one of his exercises might prove rather valuable to you as you work at improving your putting. If he is trying some long range practice putts he does not just tap in those that he missed. He takes the balls a clublength or two clublengths back and keeps putting until he has holed them all.

Whatever practice routine you use there is nothing which can compare with competition putting to sharpen your approach. If you can get a little match going on the putting green then do so. If you lose money every time you miss on the practice green you will quickly improve and you can carry that improvement on to the course when you play in a competition.

POINTS TO PONDER

When faced with a long approach putt think of putting into a three-foot bucket rather than a four-inch hole. Once you have chosen the line of putt – stick to it. Indecision on the greens causes more three putts than you might imagine.

DIFFICULT LIES AND CONDITIONS

If every shot you had to hit in golf was off a perfect lie and from a perfect position it just would not be golf. The game might be a great deal easier but it would be a great deal duller at the same time.

Part of the excitement of golf is being able, in as few strokes as possible, to get clear of trouble and, if, at times, you feel that you have been desperately unlucky with a lie in the rough keep in mind that shots off-line are meant to be punished.

When you get into difficulty on the golf course – and sometimes even the superstar golfing dollar millionaires can be seen deep in trouble – don't rush in and hit your shot as if your very life depended on it. Take time to weigh up the problems. It is at this point, more than at any other, that it pays to play the percentages.

It is when you are in the rough that intelligence must take over sheer aggression. This is the time when you may have to attack the pin from a more subtle, more circumspect circuitous route than you might otherwise have done. This is the time when you use your *head and eyes before you* reach out for a club.

THE 'IMPOSSIBLE' SHOTS

So often I've watched amateur golfers trying to 'blast out' from those diabolical spots under tree roots, below branches, in among stones without perhaps the luxury of a full swing. They stride in, confidently – wedge at the ready – to attempt to play a shot that even Severiano Ballesteros or Arnold Palmer would find difficult and might not even attempt.

In recent years no one has been better than Palmer at getting clear of the toughest rough. His strong arms, his huge wrists and massive hands have helped him thrash balls out of jungle-like territory where even other professionals, never mind amateurs, would have found it difficult to move the ball. There is a plaque erected in the rough at the sixteenth hole at Royal Birkdale where Palmer played such a fabulous recovery in the 1961 Open that the members felt there should be a permanent

Severiano Ballesteros

reminder of how the 'impossible' was once achieved.

Face up to the fact that you are not Arnold Palmer. If you contort your body into all sorts of shapes in order to get at the ball then blindly thrash at it, lunging to give extra impetus and in the process reducing club head speed, you face the possibility of a fresh air shot, passing over the top of the ball altogether.

If you do make contact you will probably hit the ball only a glancing blow and send it spinning off into deeper trouble and an even worse position. That's not only a shot wasted, it is one that could cost you a few more before the hole is finished, especially as you are now probably seething with resentment and frustration.

It is absolutely pointless to try to hit out from an impossible spot just by using brute strength so spend a moment assessing your options.

Work out how many possible escape routes you have, then eliminate them one by one as you become aware of the dangers you face. If at the end of the day you have no reasonable escape route that is when you must consider the option of a drop under penalty of one stroke within two club lengths of where your ball is lying but no nearer the hole or you can go back as far as you like as long as you keep the spot where your ball was lying between you and the flag. This sometimes puts you into a position from which you might be able to hit the green or get close to it and save your par.

How often I wonder has a golfer put an 8 or 9 down on his card and muttered ruefully: 'If only I had cut my losses and taken a drop back there in the rough.'

THE PERCENTAGE SHOTS

Assuming you can get at the ball remember that the shot you are about to play must be one which, at the very least, will get you out of trouble. If you manage to play a shot which gives you reasonable distance as well – then that is a bonus.

Don't try too much. Don't try to get clear and expect also to hit as far towards the hole as you might have hoped to, had you been playing from a perfect lie in the middle of the fairway. Attempting a dual purpose shot will often cost you strokes and not save them.

One of the classic mistakes golfers make when assessing the best shot to hit is to look *through the air* towards the target when they would be better examining the possibility of getting the ball *running* instead of flying towards the hole. Study the ground. If there is little trouble between you and the hole at ground level consider whether you would

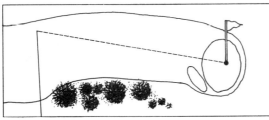

It may be wiser to play out sideways

be better advised to go down the shaft and, with a three quarter swing, play a low punched shot with an 8 iron instead of trying to fire a high recovery, with a wedge, through a five-yard gap in the trees.

I don't know how often I have seen handicap golfers try to steer the ball through a gap which is so small that their chance of making it from an even perfect lie with a perfect shot is remote. You know what I mean – a two foot square gap in the branches beckons the optimist and the foolhardy. As if mesmerised he steels himself for a Houdini-like escape shot when all he should be thinking of is devoting all his concentration to moving the ball on to the fairway in as simple a way as possible.

The result, of course, is that they hit the trees on one side or other of the gap with the ball ricocheting back into the woods and into an even worse spot. It's hardly a sensible move because now they have no chance of salvaging par. How much wiser it would have been for them to have played out sideways to give themselves a real chance of making the green with their next shot. I cannot remind you often enough that it is not how you get that ball into the hole but how many strokes you take to do it that counts. Remember balls are round. They will *roll* so use the *ground* when it suits the situation.

BALL SITTING UP

Sometimes your drive or second shot finishes in light rough with the ball sitting up on about two or three inches of grass.

Ball sitting up – beware of grounding club at address

It's just asking to be hit. This is an occasion when you could scythe right underneath the ball hitting it not forward but up in the air.

A good tip to prevent your doing this is to make sure when you address the ball that you don't place the clubhead on the ground but consciously put the club in a position immediately behind the ball. This should prevent you whipping away its imaginary feet on the way through instead of hitting it a solid blow. Again don't hit 'at it' too hard.

Slow, firm and easy does it. There is another benefit of not grounding your club in this position. If your ball moves before you hit there is no penalty but there is if you had grounded the club.

BALL LYING DOWN

If the ball is lying in deeper rough, semi-buried you will need to play a different kind of shot.

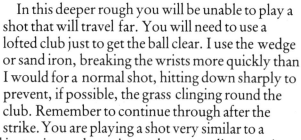

Ball sitting down – break wrists early, hit down steeply and follow through

In this deeper rough you will be unable to play a shot that will travel far. You will need to use a lofted club just to get the ball clear. I use the wedge or sand iron, breaking the wrists more quickly than I would for a normal shot, hitting down sharply to prevent, if possible, the grass clinging round the club. Remember to continue through after the strike. You are playing a shot very similar to a bunker recovery and just as it was damaging and unrewarding to quit on the shot in the sand, so it will be from this rough lie unless you carry through to a high finish. If you don't, the ball will pop up . . . and then pop down again a few yards in front of you and perhaps in even thicker grass. Try and make contact as *near* to the ball as possible.

THE 4 WOOD RECOVERY

Sometimes the rough comprises mostly heather when you might be able to use a 4 or even 5 wood to hit clear. I know the tendency from heather is to take a sharp edged club and cut through the trouble, but the wood – with the same amount of loft, but rounder head – could do the job better.

I remember in the old days at Ferndown I often played round with an early mentor of mine, Major J. S. Ruttle, a former president of the English Golf Union, the man indeed who started the Planetarium in London.

He had chronic arthritis in his hands and I was intrigued to notice, at first, that he always used his 4 wood out of the heather if the ball was lying well enough, while I would be scything away with my seven or eight iron.

'Look at my hands' he told me, when I questioned him about his club selection. 'I've not got the strength to *chop* the ball out but I can *sweep it away* with a wood. Even if I happen to top it I'll be able to move the ball at least 60 or 70 yards and that may be just enough to get me close enough to the green for a pitch and par putt. If I tried to use an iron the most I could hope to move it might be 20 yards and I might not even get it clear of the trouble.'

That is a very good lesson for us all whether we have knarled hands or not. One man on the professional tour who hits this 4 wood shot from the rough better than anyone else is Ireland's Christy O'Connor. I learned a great deal over the years watching him playing those shots and frankly I don't know why more amateur players don't use them.

If the ball is lying not too badly you can very efficiently work the ball towards the hole by gripping your 4 wood down the shaft, using plenty of wrist action and brushing your way through the heather or it might be grass – rather than cutting your way out.

LYING IN DIVOT MARKS

If you land in a divot mark in the fairway do not immediately try for a miracle recovery shot. Keep your weight on your left side during the swing, and with the hands slightly forward hit down on the ball. If you are near the green the sharper edge of an 8 or 9 iron is better than the thicker-edged wedge for this shot. If it is a deep divot and the course is

Keep weight on left side, with hands slightly forward, hit down and follow through

on clay-type soil always be willing to sacrifice distance and chop it firmly out with a 9 iron.

Most of the divot marks you will have to play out of will be facing the direction of the hole but occasionally you may come across one at right angles to your intended line of attack. In these circumstances put your weight firmly on your left foot, break those wrists earlier than normal, hit the ball from a steeper than usual angle and drive it out of the trouble.

Before you play any divot shot it always pays to spend a few seconds examining the ground to ascertain whether the divot is deep and dry or damp and sloshy. This will be a vital clue as to how to play the shot.

BARE LIES

There will be occasions when you have to play a ball off a bare lie – an area of ground where there is no grass at all or even off a tarmac road. In these circumstances you will be attempting to *sweep* the ball away without taking a divot.

Again put the weight more onto the left foot – maybe 10 per cent more than normal – steepen the swing by breaking the wrists more sharply and drive the ball forward and clear of the trouble. You are trying to brush the ball off its lie so make sure you do not collapse those wrists in the hitting area. You must keep the movement firm and decisive at all times, and above all concentrate on keeping your head steady, and swing smoothly.

WATER PROBLEMS

If your ball ends up in water on the edge of a lake or in a stream, you will probably be able to play a shot if it is not fully underneath the surface. Just remember to swing at the ball and follow through strongly because the water will slow down the clubhead speed. It's a brave shot with probably a pitching wedge and don't expect the ball to fly far. If the ball is completely underneath the surface play those percentages, do not risk a non-hit, lift out under penalty and drop on dry ground. When in water you get a false idea of 'where the ball is'. So beware, and remember to put your waterproofs on!

SPECIAL RECOVERY SHOTS

If your ball finishes in the rough close by a tree or bush from which spot it is impossible to get a stance to play right handed, don't just automatically pick up and take a drop. Consider whether or not you might be able to get clear and at the same time even move the ball forward a fair distance, playing left-handed.

If you do decide that you can get at it left-handed, turn the blade of the club – take a 8 or 9 iron which have good size heads – upside down, toe pointing downwards and grip the club left-hand below right.

You will need to be positive with the shot, swing even more slowly and more deliberately than usual. Playing left-handed might sound awkward but it can be useful to know *how to play* such a shot when the occasion arises so take some time off one afternoon on the practice ground just to play left-handed and get the feel of the swing, you may only want to hit the shot a few yards and that's not difficult.

Another alternative to left-handed shots is to play back-handed, turning your back to the direction in which you are playing and swinging the club in your right hand only, keeping the hand ahead of the ball at all times for maximum control. You'll be surprised how far you can hit it this way. Again *'try it'* in practice. If you are in the woods and feel you can get clear with an intentional fade/slice or draw/hook make sure you know you can play it before trying the shot. It is all very well watching Ballesteros or Langer bending shots round trees but this demands maximum control, skill and concentration. What you will be doing to slice intentionally is opening the face of the club, aiming left and swinging normally. To hook you will be aiming right, closing the face and using your normal swing. If you are at all uncertain about playing this shot, particularly in medal play, it is better to cut your losses and look for another way out. In match play there is less to lose.

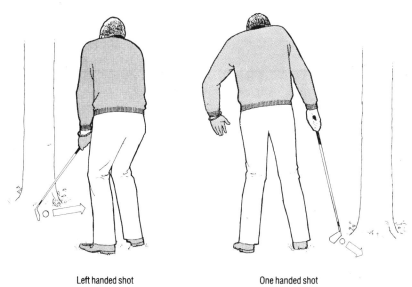

Left handed shot   One handed shot

PLAYING IN THE WIND

When the wind is blowing, make sure you use the wind to your best advantage. Far from being an enemy, the wind can be a useful ally assuming, of course, you know what you are trying to do and how best to harness it by playing the correct type of shot.

If the wind is behind you as you stand on the tee, you will feel that the opportunity to hit the ball a country mile should not be missed but don't try to take the cover off the ball by hitting it harder.

Into the wind – one club more, grip down shaft and use three quarter swing

Tee the ball slightly higher and just swing normally, maintaining your natural rhythm. Remember that the ball helped on by the wind could run much further when it lands so don't hit into trouble. If you use a driver at the hole normally you might have to go down to a 3 wood in a wind to avoid running into the rough. Playing downwind it's likely your hook or slice will straighten out a bit but the opposite is the case if you are playing into the wind.

If the wind is in your face you will be wanting to keep the ball as low as possible, using a stronger club than you would normally use for the distance you plan to hit. You will get very little roll this time because the ball will die quickly at the end of its flight. To get that extra control go two inches down the shaft. This will have the additional benefit of narrowing your swing and ensuring you hit the ball more sharply. Have the hands slightly forward for this kind of shot in order to decrease the loft and keep the hands in front right through. No need to swing fully on this one. Keep things compact by using a three-quarter backswing and three-quarter follow through.

And, of course, for shots to the green always take a club more, a 7 iron rather than your usual 8 iron. *Play within yourself.*

If the wind is blowing across the hole as you play it remember to aim up right if the wind is right to left and left if the wind is in the opposite direction. The tip is an obvious one since the ball, as it nears the end of its flight will veer off in the direction the wind is blowing. To maintain good balance widen your feet slightly more than normal for the club you are using and swing easily but decisively.

If you half-hit the ball the results in the wind could be ve damaging. Be firm, keep the body steady and let the club do the work.

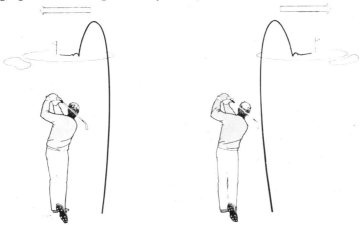

Cross winds – right to left, aim right. Left to right, aim left.

FAIRWAY BUNKERS

So many golfers try to be far too ambitious when playing out of fairway
bunkers. They have seen that great craftsman Gary Player magestically
hit 4-wood recovery shots 160 yards from the sand and think they
might be able to do the same. Before you try the shot, stop and think.
You should only be considering a wood or long iron recovery from a
trap if there is hardly any lip or bank in front of you and if the ball is
lying well. There is no use trying to play a long shot if there is a little
mound of sand *behind your ball* as it lies in the trap. If the ball is 'sitting
pretty' and if the bunker is reasonably flat remember the shot is still far
from 'easy'. You can't ground the club and that will mean you must
maintain absolute control of the shot at all times and have maximum
rhythm to pull it off. It is very difficult to hold that club just a centimetre
or two above the sand without grounding it as you prepare to hit – so
play these shots only when you are absolutely confident of the outcome.

PLAYING IN THE RAIN

It is always a good idea to have some experience of playing in the rain
especially if your ambitions in golf are to make your club side, your
county team and eventually even greater honours. You will find
yourself frequently faced with the problem of playing in bad weather
and it's best that you should know how to cope with saturated grips, a
leaking waterproof jacket and all the other miserable features of wet
weather golf as well as also having to cope with an umbrella in perhaps

windy conditions.

It may well be that you will find it best to dispense with a glove in these conditions since a soaking wet glove is virtually useless as a grip strengthener. You will have to learn how best to keep your towel dry in order to keep rubbing down wet grips and above all in bad weather you will have to work even harder at concentrating on every shot. The knowledge that your left shoe is letting in water and that rain is dripping down off your cap brim can be offputting as you line up to hit. But if you have experience of these conditions it puts you strokes, or holes, up on the opposition! I have even heard of one amateur who rigged up a shower unit in his garden so that he could practice in the 'rain'.

POINTS TO PONDER

Never rush in to play out of trouble. Take time to weigh up your options before hitting clear.

When playing from rough, remember that you want the clubhead to make as little contact with the long grass as possible, and that can only be achieved by an *upright* swing.

COMMON FAULTS

The champions in golf are the players who hit fewest bad shots, not those who hit more spectacular shots than anyone else. If you can cut down the number of bad shots you hit in a round then you are well along the path towards improving your game.

Most bad shots can be put down to one of half a dozen basic faults. If you top a fairway wood or slice a drive or hook an approach or smother a pitch or shank an iron you will have hit a shot from the common fault category. The fewer common fault shots you hit, the better your score.

Getting out of trouble by deliberately hooking or slicing the ball is quite different from hitting slices or hooks indiscriminately on the course because you do not know how to correct the fault . . . or, if you do, are unwilling to take steps to cure your problem.

HOOKING

It's scarcely a compliment to be known as a hooker, especially if you are a lady! The hook is a very destructive shot. It can get you into some impossible situations. There are many golfers playing off single figure handicaps who, time after time, crumple under medal or match-play pressure and start to hook. I have often come across a 10 handicap player who wants to get rid of his violent hook, but not at the expense of changing his grip. He is showing four or even five knuckles on that left hand and with his right hand strongly under the shaft he feels *comfortable*. His handicap has been achieved despite his grip and probably because he has a brilliant short game. He wants to improve but he has no hope unless he gets his hands right. Many young people do not take up golf at an early age because they prefer to be involved in more active team sports like rugby and soccer – contact sports in which they can get rid of some of their pent up energy. In golf they can't. In golf they must remain in control of themselves at all times or fail. These youngsters may not turn to golf until they are in their late 30's when the pace of football or rugby is too much for them. It is only when they realise just how much they have been missing but their switch over is

Left: the hooker's swing – inside to out   Right: the hooker's stance – too closed

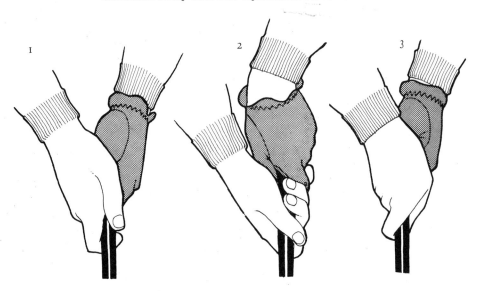

Check that grip   1 Correct   2 Hooker's   3 Slicer's

too casual. Because they have a certain *ball sense* they are quite capable of hitting reasonably well despite a bad grip. They can improve up to a point.

Since the foundation of their swing is suspect there is, not unnaturally, a limit to the improvement they can achieve. They might get down to 12 handicap but then further improvement can only be made by altering to a more orthodox grip, one which will produce a more reliable swing.

If you come into this category it may mean sacrificing *comfort* but rather than live with that hook why not make the grip change at the end of the season during the winter months when scoring is maybe less important? It may not be easy to make the alteration but it would be worth it. Unhappily, too often the golfer with this problem is not prepared to make the change.

If you have a tendency to hook or slice to such an extent that your golf game is constantly spoiled by these wild shots it might not be your grip that is at fault. It might just be simply a question of alignment or body position or ball position or simply your inability to control the clubface during the swing. All these faults can be cured much more simply than having to change your whole game by learning to play with a new grip and new swing pattern.

The simple way to discover what might be causing the hook is to go through a check list rather like a pilot cross checks his instruments before he takes off in his jumbo jet. Check first that the right hand has not slipped underneath the shaft, 'strengthening' the grip. If you can see more than two and a half knuckles on your left hand your grip is too strong.

Next, check your stance and ensure that you have not moved to a 'closed' position, that is, a stance with the left foot in front of the right. If you have you will be coming back too far *inside* and will have a tendency to hook the club head in the hitting area as you fight to square up. The line of your stance should be slightly left of target. You can check this easily enough by laying a club along your feet. If that line is square to target or is heading off right then that might be encouraging you to swing with an *in-to-out* action, a hooking action. So aim the club just *left* of the target and all else should follow on naturally.

SLICING

Slicing can be so demoralising you might even consider giving up the game altogether. There's nothing more frustrating than hitting the ball hard yet losing 40 to 50 yards because of a vicious slice, surely the most punishing shot in golf.

Yet it might take only a very small correction, not necessarily a grip change, to get you hitting the ball straight or at least straighter. It needs only a very small alteration to have you hitting the fairways and not scrambling about in the rough.

If the reason for your hook was an *inside* to *outside* swing then the reason for the slice is a swing coming from *outside to in*, chopping across the ball. This can be caused because your grip is too weak and it's too weak if there's only one knuckle showing on that left hand – there must be two.

Once again wrong alignment could be the cause of the trouble. This time your stance will be too open – slicers *always* over compensate. You want to stand ever so slightly open but take care. If you overdo this you will take the club back well outside the line and come back on a line that only succeeds in cutting the ball away right. Fast hand action from this position makes things worse.

The third way you can slice is by having the clubface open at impact.

Left: the slicer's swing – outside to in Right: the slicer's stance – too open

This can be caused by getting the hands ahead of the ball as you try to delay the hit the way the professionals do.

Chronic slicers far outnumber hookers – perhaps by six to one – and my best advice is to encourage them to go to their professional for a course of lessons. Unfortunately, too many keen golfers just live with their slices and hooks. There's certainly no disgrace in having lessons so long as you are serious about them! He will 'line you up' and that will cure the dreaded slice so, *do it today.*

TOPPING

Some golfers find their *bête noire* on the golf course is an inability to hit a clean crisp fairway wood. Instead of sending the ball 180 yards on towards the flag they send it scuttling just 50 yards along the ground or they drive it into the earth as if they were hitting a tent peg with a massive hammer.

Basically, what you are doing if you have this golfing 'disease' is trying to *scoop* the ball away, leaning to the right as you come into the hitting area and sending the clubhead up and almost over the ball. Other reasons for topping are a tendency to crouch too much over the ball, bending the left arm at impact or moving the head.

This is how I would go about correcting the fault. Stand up to the ball, maintain your height, don't dip up and down but rhythmically use the arms to sweep the shot away, using if necessary a 4 or 5 wood instead of the 2 or 3 wood you had probably planned to use.

I can never understand why golfers persist always in playing the most difficult club in any situation. Maybe they have been conditioned into believing they are breaking the rules by playing a club other than the one specifically designed to hit a certain kind of shot a certain distance. That is muddled thinking.

If you are mis-hitting a 3 wood off the fairway time after time switch to a 4 wood or even a 5 wood if you have one in the bag. You will find you will hit the ball almost as far and, more importantly, you will consequently boost your confidence to the point when you can return to the 3 wood and use it successfully.

Guy Wolstenholme, the former Walker Cup amateur and top professional now based in Australia, is one of the great fairway wood artists in modern professional golf. He frequently uses his driver off the turf sending the ball away very impressively. He thinks only of hitting *the top half of the ball* on these shots – the very thing the high handicap player is mentally trying to avoid. In other words he is sweeping the

95

Guy Wolstenholme, playing a driver off the fairway | Nick Faldo, another fine exponent of the fairway wood

shot away. I cannot stress too much the importance of cultivating this sweeping feeling.

HEAD-UP

One of the most common of the common faults is 'head up' – at least that's what golfers usually exclaim when one of their partners plays a bad shot. In fact what has really happened is that the head has moved because the body has moved. One of the keys to good golf is to keep your body still throughout the shot – remember our windmill.

We want as many *non-moving parts* as we can in our swing in order to cut down the risk of error – it is rather like a bicycle chain with too many links. It will work all right for a while but then the slack chain will come off – usually at the worst possible time. So it is with too loose a golfing swing so tighten it up by eliminating sway and if you do you should have no trouble keeping your head still and your eyes on the ball.

HITTING FROM THE TOP

This refers to the movement at the top of the backswing which pushes the weight back on the right foot and throws the whole swing off balance. Most of us like to hit the ball hard but it will never be achieved by forcing. Hitting from the top occurs when you start that downswing too quickly, concentrating the built-up energy in the top half of the downswing instead of the bottom half – the half where you need the power to hit the ball. Swing your arms freely and if you have difficulty in controlling the hands at the start of the downswing it may be some consolation to realise that this was Jack Nicklaus' big problem in his early days as well.

His cure was to think of the first half of that movement down as one that should be achieved at the same speed as the last half of the upswing. It helped him keep those hands in control at all times and that is what you are trying to do. Feel 'the pace' of the swing.

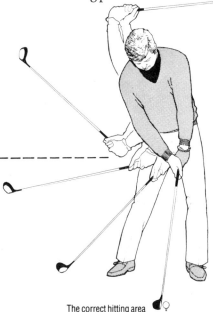

SHANKING

No shot in golf is more shattering and causes more anguish than the shank – indeed it is such a worrying feature of the game that golfers shrink from mentioning it, whispering about it under their breath. Many superstitious golfers regard it as the golfing equivalent of the plague. They

The correct hitting area

believe it can be passed by word of mouth from player to player – or even by example. Most clubs have noted 'shankers' who just need to see or hear about a shank on an adjoining fairway to start them off. Some feel they may even be carriers of the 'disease'.

Shanking or socketing is, as the terms imply, hitting the ball with the shank or socket rather than with the face of the clubhead – so that it flies off almost at right angles.

I have been lucky in my golfing career to have shanked only twice – on both occasions from bunkers when I had the clubface well open at address, playing from downhill lie, but I know of professionals who have suffered the shanks throughout their careers. Just when it seems they have conquered the problem they flash one off to the right and no shot is more of a confidence-crumbler than that!

Peter Thomson shanked quite often when he was at the peak of his career and I remember Dai Rees shanking at Troon in the 1950 Open when in contention to win the title, finally won by Bobby Locke. He used that double-handed grip, of course, and sometimes it was rather loose and open at the top so perhaps that was to blame for possibly the

Ball too near right foot and club face closed as it comes into the ball

Hands too far forward and club face too open as it comes into the ball

costliest shank of his long and distinguished career. Most shanks happen on approach shots with an 8 or 9 iron or a wedge although, heaven preserve them, some unfortunates have been known to shank every iron in the bag. My father had a theory that shanking was caused by one of only two things – either the blade was so open that you could not help but hit the ball off the pipe or that the face was so shut the ball was squeezed out the side as if being put through a rolling mill. He called this the rolling shank but the more usual shank is the open-faced variety.

Most players shank because they are standing with their right foot too near the ball. As a result they either close the face on the ball as they hit so that the neck of the club hits the ball first, or they open the face, keep it open and jab at it because they cannot get a proper swing at it. The right shoulder comes over the top, closes the face, and bingo!

There is, I am sorry to say, no magic cure for shanking. You may have been told to 'just swing more slowly' next time and to 'move back just a little'. You might have been advised to put your weight on the balls of your feet and 'sit back' to hit the shot or to put the weight on your heels so that you must consciously lean forward but here is what I would do if I caught a dose of the dreaded shanks.

I would try, more consciously, to put my feet *underneath* my body so that I would neither be reaching for it nor be too close to the ball. The object of this would be to regain that *feel* which I had clearly lost when I shanked. I would be trying to regain rhythm, confidence, balance. You know it all sounds so easy yet sadly it's not – but keep trying.

POINTS TO PONDER

If you are a slicer consciously play for the right side of the fairway, and concentrate on hitting past your chin, with a good follow-through.

Never stretch for the ball. If you have to, then you are too far from it. Move a little closer and stand comfortably.

GETTING INTO TRIM

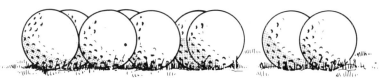

Why does Nikki Lauda climb into his racing car and spend a week getting to know a racetrack before he lines up for a Grand Prix? Why does top operatic singer Joan Sutherland set aside time each morning for an hour of vocal acrobatics? Why does Yehudi Menuhin keep his fingers supple with regular exercises and repeated runs up and down the scale on his violin?

They all practice because it is an essential ingredient of their success, indeed their continuing success in their chosen professions. So it is in golf. Proper practice can help you improve and maintain that improvement.

I have impressed upon you earlier the importance, indeed the necessity, to hit a few practice shots before you tee off just to warm up but don't forget that the practice ground, if your club is lucky enough to have one, is there all the time to be used sensibly by *you*.

PLAN YOUR PRACTICE

An hour on the practice ground with a properly prepared schedule can do your game a tremendous amount of good without leaving you exhausted, your hands bleeding from the punishment and your muscles aching.

A proper schedule – that is important. If your set routine is too demanding then it might do your game positive harm. The effort you are making on the practice ground must be channelled to maximum benefit and a word of advice – never be put off by those who suggest that practising is somehow un-British or by those who label you 'pot-hunter' because you take trouble to practice. If more golfers took just a little time to practice they would improve their game and their enjoyment of it. The plain fact is that most people are just too lazy.

In the early 1950s Max Faulkner had a practice bag of 100 balls and was hammering away, down on his farm, hitting 700 balls and milking 84 cows a day to strengthen his wrists. This schedule suited him but it was no use for me.

I never was a great practiser but I always took the view that I could learn more hitting 12 balls sensibly than 120 stupidly.

You cannot maintain concentration if you are pumping balls indiscriminately into the far distance but you can if you are using just a few balls and making every shot count – 12 drives, 12 5-iron shots, 12 bunker recoveries. Incidentally, if your club does not have practice ground markers set your own target and aim for that every time. This will create interest and stop you trying to out-hit yourself with every shot.

Make sure you have fairly decent balls, which you will have used to play a few rounds but which do not have great big 'smiles' on the covers. Those smiles or cuts will affect the flight and give you a false idea of how you are hitting the ball.

Keep the balls reasonably clean because this will help you find them when you come to collect them. It is very time-wasting, not to say, frustrating, to have to look for balls on the practice range so put *your* mark on *your* balls to avoid confusion if the practice range is busy.

MAINTAIN CONCENTRATION

Although you may find it a bit of a fag to walk backwards and forwards picking up just a dozen balls this is not really wasted effort. This is all part of the slowing down process, a process designed to help you get the rhythm right and to help you concentrate better when you are actually hitting the shots.

I don't know how many times I have been out giving a lesson to someone who hit the first two tubefuls of balls badly but then did quite well on the third tubeful. That was the time to stop but in the few minutes remaining of the lesson the pupil, endeavouring to get value for money, hit a fourth tubeful on the run and consequently badly.

At the end there was the inevitable groan of despair, the forlorn cry that he or she had almost got it right near the end, only to lose it all again in the last five minutes. Well, of course, it had to happen. The last few shots were hit with tired muscles and without proper concentration. Guard against such action.

Most people practise badly. They start off with such good intentions. They have read that you should always take a preliminary swing (maybe even two), hit the ball, watch it carefully in flight, watch where it lands, take three deep breaths, look around like a cricketer surveying the outfield, bring up the next ball, have a couple of swings . . . and so on.

That is fine but within 20 minutes these same people are moving so fast that it seems as if they have two or three balls in the air at the one time. All the good intentions have disappeared. They never can hope to get anything right and often stagger back to the clubhouse convinced they will never ever improve or even that they might be better giving up the game.

When I practised, in my tournament days, I was in the habit of using a 9 iron to start, then worked through the bag to the driver using the odd numbered clubs. This produced a nice balance of shots.

PRACTICE WITH INTENT

If your fault is a really bad one make sure you get professional advice, otherwise all the practice you do might be of little use in helping you improve. You might be compounding the fault or trying to correct something you have not even got wrong while not making the alteration needed to change what you have got wrong. So seek advice.

The practice range is not just there for the luxury of hitting long irons and slamming woods into the far distance. It is there for you to practise all length shots from a reasonably level lie. That does not mean you can't hit shots from more awkward lies and from the rough as well. Playing shots from the rough, in fact, can be invaluable if you are one of golf's unhappy 'quitters' because the resistance of the grass will force you to follow through just to get the ball away.

All this may sound rather obvious but you would be surprised how few golfers know how to use the practice ground and the area around it properly.

One of the greatest practisers of golf is Gary Player who practised as much as the great Ben Hogan did 30 years ago. It is only recently that Player has cut down dramatically on the length of his sessions. He practises before he goes out and, whenever he has completed his round, signed, cross-checked his card and handed in his score, he is off again to the practice range for the session he calls the most helpful of all.

Helpful – because you should not be experimenting before the round, you should just be warming up . . . leaving the experimenting and correcting of any faults that have cropped up during your play until after you have finished.

Other golfers hardly need to practise at all. The greatest modern example of a non-practiser is Johnny Miller who knows his swing so well that he can sit in an armchair in front of the fire of an evening, make any necessary alterations mentally, then put them into practice with a couple of hits on the practice ground the following day. Miller is exceptional.

PRACTICE FACILITIES

One of the things that makes proper practising difficult in this country is the great lack of adequate practice facilities. Some clubs have only a small bit of field as a practice ground, but even this is better than nothing.

The other big fault is that while new sand is constantly being spread in the on-course bunkers, some golf club committees never think of looking after the practice bunker which becomes an unused wilderness of weeds and hard clay. It doesn't make sense.

Keep your club committee conscious of the need to provide facilities of some description – even a net – if none exist and if you do have facilities make sure your club looks after them properly.

If you have no practice area – and wouldn't it be nice to have a 250,000 dollar circular practice area such as the one Nicklaus has built himself at Muirfield Village in Ohio – you can use your course to practise on from time to time, if it is quiet. Don't let me hear you bleating that you never get a chance to play long iron shots because your course has a surfeit of drive and pitch holes.

Greg Norman

103

There is a simple solution to this. If your first hole is 300 yards long, stand just off the first tee and play your opening shot with a wedge, hitting the ball some 80 yards up the fairway. Now you are faced with having to play a 3 or 4 iron second shot to a smallish green . . . or a 3 wood . . . or perhaps a lay-up shot, then a hopeful pitch and putt for par?

I had to do that at Parkstone where they had five par 5 holes which were unreachable in two, five short holes all about 5 iron range and eight drive and pitch holes. I often played the course the wrong way round.

TRY ON EVERY SHOT

If you are practising on the course there is another lesson you should learn – I learned it from my father at Ferndown. Sometimes on the tenth green I would have a putt of two to two and a half feet for my par, move quickly to tap it in and miss it. When I finished I would be asked what I had scored and would be describing my 68 to him, when he would ask, almost casually, what I had taken at the tenth – adding pointedly that he had been watching me through the binoculars and that he thought I had missed a shortish putt there.

I would stammer out some sort of explanation, adding that if I had really tried on that putt I would have holed it, but he would simply cut me off in mid sentence.

'You are only kidding yourself . . . you should never do that', he would say.

Golf is almost a complete mirror of one's character and it is a great character builder, so never fool yourself out on the course. Even if it is a practice round try on every shot. That's what Jack Nicklaus does all the time and he has topped three millions in golf dollar earnings.

PRACTICE AT HOME

Practice need not necessarily be done at the club. You probably know of golfers who have putting improvers, so that they can practise those six to eight footers on their carpets. But there's a lot more that you can do. I know of golfers who have rigged up nets in their gardens or their garages and maybe even a floodlight of some description to allow them to hit balls all the year round . . . and at night. Remember to choose a small mesh net or you might just drive through it and put a ball through the window of your next door neighbour. That could be costly!

The garden or garage routine is ideal if you are afraid to swing indoors for fear of breaking a light fitting or that ornament grannie gave you as a wedding present although you wish she hadn't.

If the garage is big enough that has certain advantages over the garden since a little paraffin stove can keep you warm on the cold winter nights – but that is a refinement you do not necessarily require.

I am a great believer in a net. It is certainly no substitute for the practice range, for accurately letting you know where your shots will finish but you can get the feel of the shot and you can appreciate whether or not the ball left the middle of the club or not. Getting that feel, as I have said before, is so important. It's all to do with balance and rhythm and tempo and there is not much difference between the last two, if anything.

It's interesting, you know, how many fellows play golf so rhythmically and yet who walk in a rather ungainly way. Take Tom Weiskopf, a golfer with magestic rhythm, and a swing unmatched for technical excellence in America today, but who has a most unathletic walk.

Have you ever noticed how Hale Irwin, who has such a polished compact technique walks with short little jerky steps or how Gary Player, with his long arms, has a long loping stride.

Arnold Palmer is more rhythmical when he walks but there are very few golfers who move with the grace with which they hit their shots. There are not many golfers like Don January or Kel Nagle who hit shots with ease and 'stroll' round the course.

LOOKING FOR TEMPO

The important secret of tempo is the ability to hit the ball at just the right moment, packing the punch at just the right second on the middle of the club face. It should be rather like one of Henry Cooper's left hooks which travelled just nine inches but which crunched on an opponent's jaw. Just as Henry knew he had landed flush on target – his opponent was probably on the canvas to underline the fact – so you can always tell when you have hit the golf ball properly. Even professionals hit few perfect shots in a round but when they do they will probably put them down, in a word, to tempo.

Never try to scoop at the ball. If your body is in the right position just return the clubhead to the ball, hit past your chin, releasing the clubhead and sweep the ball away rhythmically – this will help build up tempo.

It is interesting to watch older golfers who suffer perhaps from a spot of rheumatism. They just plonk their feet down, use a three quarter backswing and hit the ball foward with maximum balance and rhythm.

They frequently score better than those whizz kids who want to take the cover off the ball by hitting it super hard and frequently end up hammering the clubhead into the ground because they lack rhythm.

You will need to work at it on the practice ground but you will know when your tempo is right because you will hit clean, crisp shots.

Everyone must find his own tempo. Arnold Palmer's tempo is very different from Sam Snead's, Gary Player's is different from that of Brian Barnes and so on. But these great players have one thing in common. They look different, their swing speed varies, but they all swing smoothly and rhythmically. Admittedly, tempo is an elusive quality. Some people find it for a few holes and often lose it when they have to play a pressure shot – for example, when their opponent has laid his approach a foot from the flag. What often happens is the player under pressure flashes at the shot – he forgets to complete his backswing. Maintain your tempo and try to regard the pressure shot as you would any other shot.

Always complete that backswing

IN THE WIND

If you are thinking of going out to practise when it is blowing a gale my advice is: stay in the clubhouse. If you do go out you will find practising uncomfortable and more than likely it will be cold and you will have to wrap up so much you will be totally unable to swing properly anyway. There's nothing like a wind for losing tempo.

Make this rule – practise only in the wind if you specifically want to practise wind shots or if you are in desperate need of a massive morale booster. You can get that by teeing the ball up high and driving downwind. If you hit quietly and smoothly you will send the ball as far as Nicklaus or Jacklin in calm conditions and it will make you feel good, but more often than not indiscriminate practising in the wind can do harm to your swing and shatter rhythm.

EXERCISE AND FITNESS

There is a great deal you can do indoors to help improve your golf without swinging a club. You can strengthen your wrists and hands by squeezing little rubber balls just like Henry Cotton does or you can buy a little hand exerciser which does the same job.

I finished playing golf seriously some time ago and my left wrist has shrunk in girth about an inch. I used to fasten my watch strap at the last notch. Now I fasten it at the first and the watch still hangs loose.

There are golfers who do twenty to thirty press-ups a day to strengthen their arms and legs but there is no need to be too Tarzan-like in your endeavours. Gary Player once had to pull out of an important championship because he cricked his neck while doing an unusually acrobatic exercise in his bath. Exercise prudently.

Bob Charles is a great believer in jogging to keep his legs strong and himself super fit for tournaments. You will often see him, and maybe Australian Graham Marsh, set off on an evening run even if they are staying in the middle of a busy city. Another 'runner' is Player who has been known to sprint backwards and forwards along many a well-carpeted hotel corridor when unwilling to jostle with the traffic and pedestrians in the streets outside. Sam Snead has kept himself fit over the years and this has been as vital a factor as that superb swing for his staying so long at the top in international golf. Even in his late sixties Sam was so super-supple that he could kick the lintel above an ordinary door, kicking as high as 6 feet 6 inches. If you are unimpressed, just try it yourself but watch you don't overbalance and break your neck.

You will play better golf if you are fit but I sometimes wonder if some of our younger golfers on the professional tour appreciate this. Some are a stone or even more overweight – it must be the good life that does it. How much better golfers would be if they shed that extra poundage? For one thing there would be less strain on the legs – and strong legs really are so important in golf.

Whatever way you decide to keep yourself fit make sure you persevere and that applies equally to practising. It is rather like dieting. You love chips and ice cream and it is very easy to take a portion of each today and plan to start the diet tomorrow.

Your game is bound to improve if you just spend a little time keeping the hands supple and maintain a nice easy smooth swing but don't become a bore about training to the extent that you disrupt the household and eventually family life. Golf, after all, is only a game.

POINTS TO PONDER
On the practice ground try to improve head steadiness by hitting a series of shots, and each time staring momentarily at your divot after you have hit the shot.

Always warm up with the easiest clubs, the short irons.

GETTING INTO GEAR

If you are just starting in golf you do not have to ask that all-too-patient bank manager for a loan in order to equip yourself properly. Of course, if you were to decide you needed only the best clubs, the most expensive golf bag (I once saw one made of crocodile skin), mink head covers, cashmere sweaters, expensive shoes you could run up a somewhat frightening account but there is no need to be so lavish. Second-hand clubs for the beginner are more than satisfactory. They may not be tailor-made to your build and swing but such refinements can come later when your game has improved to the extent that you want to go on to higher things.

Sometimes in a back corner of an uncle's house you may come across an old set of clubs which you could use to see whether or not you like the game but which, in the long run, might prove unsatisfactory.

Don't throw them away, however. They may become valuable as golfing antiques. There is quite a thriving trade these days in old clubs and other Victorian golfing paraphernalia, with enthusiasts buying up discarded old equipment, not just to display in glass cases on walls but to sell at good prices.

There is quite a craze at the moment for old Tommy Armour woods in the United States – the ones made between 1946 and 1955. Frankly, some of the heads on these clubs are over-rated but that is of little concern to the bargain hunters, because they are after the now very rare wood persimmon, which can be reshaped if necessary. Tom Weiskopf has been collecting them and Johnny Miller has at least fifty, worth over a hundred dollars each.

BUYING YOUR FIRST CLUBS

If you are buying your first new half set I would strongly advise you at this stage to ignore the driver. Buy instead a 3 wood for use off the tee and a 4 or 5 wood for fairway shots. Woods are easier to hit – one reason why some golfers carry a full set of wooden clubs, even up to the equivalent of the pitching wedge.

As for irons, get a 3 iron, a 5, 7 and 9 iron, a sand wedge and a sensible putter. As you improve and your pocket will allow you can always augment that half set with other clubs from the same model. Don't wait too long, however, as golf club models are like cars they change, regularly, although most sets remain on the market for at least five years. The beauty about buying a matched half set is that if you end up not liking golf (or if it does not like you) you have a saleable commodity – but enough of this despondency. Of course you will enjoy playing the game!

NEW IDEAS AND EQUIPMENT

Many modern irons are described by the makers as heel and toe models, a reference to the fact that the weight in the clubhead is more evenly distributed in order to reduce the odds of a golfer hitting a bad shot. The spreading of the weight makes for a bigger *sweet spot* on the club face and, therefore, there is less chance of a wicked slice or hook when you fail to hit the ball properly.

At least that is the claim, and I have no doubt that it works very well for many people. As far as I am concerned, however, I stick by the traditional club which has stood the test of time, the club which has the weight towards the centre of the club face. Heel and toe is losing popularity in the United States. More traditional models are again in favour and that is significant, for all golfing trends these days seem to start on the other side of the Atlantic.

It is often said that there is nothing new in golf and certainly most of the gimmicks which manufacturers bring out these days – with the exception of course of new material – have been tried before with probably less high-powered publicity and advertising campaigns.

It might be fair to suggest that the really good ideas become standard, but that the gimmicky ones die quickly only to blossom again years later. Golfers really are the most susceptible of sportsmen to the hard and the soft sell. They are prepared to believe in anything if they think that it will benefit their golf, but I do advise you to examine some of the more high-flown claims and ask yourself seriously if your own golf can *really* benefit from some new piece of equipment.

I can easily illustrate what I mean by instancing the two balls on the market – the indestructible one that you just cannot cut and the unloseable one – illegal in competitions but all right for practice rounds – which sends up a built in radio signal which you can pick up on a small receiver in your pocket. That's fine in theory but if you hit your indestructible ball or your unloseable one into a six-foot deep lake in the middle of your course there is precious little you can do about it. I suppose the ball would remain indestructible under water or continue to send out its signal sending the trout into raptures!

You may be wondering as you set off to buy that first set or half set of clubs whether or not you should be investing in a graphite.

The big advantage of graphite is that because it is very light – lighter

Tommy Horton with his graphite driver

than the traditional steel shaft – you are able, potentially, to hit the ball a bit further. Many tournament professionals with very wristy styles certainly do like Christy O'Connor and Tommy Horton.

In America, Gene Littler, still one of the great stylists in golf, plays a full set of graphite-shafted clubs since his major chest operation, using the graphite to compensate for his lack of muscle. When Johnny Miller won the Open at Royal Birkdale in 1976 he used a full set of graphites but has not used them again, although he does continue to hit tee shots with uncanny accuracy using a graphite-shafted driver. On the European circuit little Manuel Pinero has had a great deal of success with his full set of graphites. The claim that graphite, because it is lighter, is more easy to swing is offset in my mind by the fact that with many graphite clubs the shaft twists more – there's more torque – adding a further movement for you to worry about. I believe it can be more difficult to control a graphite-shafted club for this reason. It's a club you must swing slowly and with a great deal of rhythm. A bad shot with a bad graphite club can be a really destructive one. Yet it is fair perhaps to add that the most improved graphite shaft on the market now has, it is claimed, less torque than steel. Maybe it is significant that Jack Nicklaus, who must have tried graphite clubs, does not use them in tournaments. Neither does Gary Player – or should I say he does not appear to use graphite. His clubs are so bandaged and taped up at times that it is difficult to know just what clubs he has in his bag!

Graphite undoubtedly is more popular and will be more enduring than aluminium was a few years back, but for the average golfer I think it is best to stick to clubs with shafts made of light-weight steel – it is being improved all the time and it is becoming lighter and lighter. If you want to try a graphite driver, most professionals have a couple in the back shop which they will hire out at around £1 a time. You might need a couple of trials before you decide but no doubt the professional will be happy to oblige. He does not want to have unhappy customers. It is not in his interests to sell you something with which he feels you might not be happy in the long term – that's bad business. He will be quite content to let you take your time in deciding.

A recent development, much favoured by some tour professionals, is the new style metal wood – like graphite clubs lightweight and designed to help you hit the ball further. This is the new luxury club which might put you one up on your golfing chums. If it also works that is an added bonus.

WHAT KIND OF SHAFTS?

Assuming you stick with light-weight steel you will want a slightly stiffish shaft, not a whippy one as many people advocate. It is argued often that whippy shafts can help generate power in the hitting area but they are less easy to control than the shaft which is slightly stiff. Anything whippy – like a fishing rod – encourages a swishing motion and it takes a pair of educated hands to transform that into a swing. The really good amateurs, of course, and the professionals often use extra stiff shafts since the pros generate so much power coming into the hitting area, but that is no good for the average amateur. He needs only slight stiffness and a light shaft – and that lightness is important because that can give you the speed more reliably than the whip of the whippy shaft. You have often heard people say, I am sure, that the shafts on the American clubs which you can buy from the professionals are better than ours, that they have more 'life' and I think that assumption is quite correct.

The reason is that the Americans, I am sure, upgrade their shafts so that the regular becomes stiff, the stiff extra stiff and so on. They take an ounce or so off the headweight and make the grips *standard thickness throughout,* instead of thicker for the left hand than right as ours are. The result is good feel and it surprises me that more manufacturers do not appear to have followed this trend. You will be mesmerised sometimes by all the talk of swing weight in fully matched sets of clubs – that is, the relationship between the weight of the clubshaft and that of the clubhead. I think this is a bit misleading since the real relationship of these two weights can only really be judged when the club is being swung. This static weight relationship is of little help.

When Hagen was in his heyday he played with a bag of mixed clubs of all different swing weights and there are golfers on the American and European tour doing very well at the moment with clubs which feel good although they are not matched. 'Feel' is still a big part of good golf.

THE ROLE OF THE CLUB PROFESSIONAL

When you are buying your new clubs get the advice of a professional. Let him help you out. Age, height, weight, even sex, comes into golf! Everyone's shape and size is different and just as I would not expect my suits to fit my next door neighbour I don't expect my golf clubs to suit him either. If you are a member of a club, it really is in your interests, and his, to support your pro.

Think of your club professional as your tailor. You may be lucky and get something off the peg or shelf at just the right price or it may be best to have clubs tailor-made for you. Anything is possible. If you are a lightweight with small wrists your professional may recommend men's clubs with ladies shafts and they can be made up *if you are prepared to wait*. And a word for the ladies on this subject. Do not be satisfied with your husband's cast-off clubs. Men's clubs are usually too heavy and too long for women. You will swing a lot more sweetly with proper ladies' clubs.

On this subject of size and build it has always intrigued me how few great golfers are over 6 feet tall. There is Tom Weiskopf, a former British Open winner, a golfing dollar millionaire, a man with probably the best swing in America at the moment, full of rhythm and style. There is the massive George Archer who won the U.S. Masters. There is Peter Oosterhuis and there is, of course, Johnny Miller, but they all belong to a very select band. Most of the golfing greats have been between 5 feet 7 inches and 6 feet tall. Nicklaus, Hogan, Thomson, Player, Locke, Trevino, Watson all come into that ideal height range. I do not know why this should be so, except that I suspect it is in some way related to balance and alignment, and swing plane.

GOLF BALLS

Golf balls are now an expensive commodity and the range is wide enough for you to choose the best bargain, but again study the claims of the manufacturers. As an amateur you can use the small ball (1·62 inches diameter) and in British conditions I think that this is best for you. If you hope to become a top amateur and in time a professional you would be advised to persevere, however, with the big ball (1·68 inches in diameter), the one used on all professional circuits and stipulated these days for most major amateur events as well.

At club level, sales of big balls are a very small percentage of a pro's ball turnover, and it is easy to realise why. The argument that by playing the bigger ball you will become a better striker (because any mistakes are exaggerated) in the long run is fine, but most amateurs are interested primarily in long hitting and in British type weather conditions it is the small ball that behaves best to let you achieve this.

All balls, big and small, come in various compressions which is all to do with the way the inner part of the ball (it is not solid) has been wound, or, if it is solid, how hard or soft the inside is.

The higher the compression of the ball the harder you must hit it to

114

make it operate effectively or, if you like, to force it out of shape and fly away off the clubhead fast. It sounds very appealing, but not many handicap golfers can successfully use this hard ball. It is much easier for amateurs to use the low compression type which compresses more easily on impact and flies with more elasticity, perhaps not so far but with a comparatively easy swing.

BEGINNER'S SHOPPING LIST

Along with clubs and balls there are several other basic necessities. A golf bag, obviously, and I strongly advise you to get one that is fairly light, with a large pocket for waterproofs and an extra pullover, a small pocket for balls and tees, and a fitting on the outside of the bag for an umbrella.

A trolley to carry your clubs is not an absolute necessity but well worth having. What is very important is a good pair of golf shoes. If you are going to be out on that course for over three hours you want to look after your feet.

Most golfers, nowadays, wear a glove on their left hand and I think that it is a very good investment as it gives the grip a feeling of greater security.

A golfing bag cover or alternatively a bag flap is essential to protect the clubheads when you are travelling and the flap, when tucked in, can also keep the rain from seeping down to the grips on a wet day on the course.

Left: the basics Right: the extras

CARE OF EQUIPMENT

Clubs and equipment are expensive and they must be looked after. Buy headcovers for the woods for protection and if you are unlucky enough to find yourself caught in a heavy shower of rain make sure you *dry the clubs* before you stick them back in the boot of the car.

Take the trouble occasionally to give your irons a thorough clean with soap and water, not only to smarten their appearance but also to get rid of that mud and dirt which clogs up those all-so-important grooves on the clubface. Check the spikes on your golf shoes regularly and replace those that are missing or are worn down.

I said at the beginning that equipping yourself need not be all that costly – indeed, beginners can be kitted out for less than a hundred pounds, even in these days of inflation, but it is really worth while taking out an insurance policy for loss or breakage.

Once you have got started, you will no doubt want to acquire some of the accessories that your golfing friends may already possess – natty headgear, colourful waterproofs, the latest in slacks and sweaters. Golfers naturally like to keep up with the Joneses and why not? There is that old adage that if you want to feel like a golfer and play like one you must look the part.

Winston Churchill is reputed to have described golf as being a game devised by the devil and played with implements ill adapted for the purpose. Maybe that was true in the old days but not now. Golfers today cannot use inadequate equipment as their excuse for poor play.

POINTS TO PONDER

Check that the size of your grips matches the size of your hands.

If you are an older golfer or a long handicap player consider discarding that 2 or 3 iron in favour of a 5 wood.

RULES AND ETIQUETTE

Like every other game golf requires more than skill and equipment. The order and method of play is governed by a complicated set of rules and the manner in which the game is played is equally governed by an unwritten code of conduct.

THE R & A

The rules of golf – and there are 41 of them framed to try to make the game as fair as possible – are so complex that dozens of queries are answered every month from all over the world at golf's headquarters – the Royal and Ancient Golf Club of St Andrews.

It is from St Andrews that golf throughout the world, with the notable exception of America and Canada, is controlled and the rules' posers flood in from countries as far apart as Australia and Iceland, Tobago and Zambia, as well, of course, from Britain.

Much of the work is repetitive and answers to recurring problems can be sent back by return. Frequently a problem which has cropped up in New Zealand is similar to one dealt with for the Kenya Golf Union months earlier and the same query could crop up a few weeks later after an incident in Spain.

Annual decisions on the rules are circulated worldwide and translated into several languages but snags can occasionally occur in the translation. A few years ago in Italy a local golfer cleared away enough sand in a bunker to make sure that the ball he was about to hit was in fact his. He was breaking the rule which permits you only to make sure a ball is there before you play it. Afterwards if you find it is not your ball then there is no penalty and you can go back and hunt again in the sand for the correct one.

In the English original the rule was quite clear, but in the free translation into Italian there was an ambiguity about how much sand could be brushed away.

The really tricky problems are dealt with by an R & A Rules Committee who can assess the seriousness of a breach, if there has been

117

one, and use a certain logic to match up the decision with others of a similar nature in order to achieve a reasonable balance of consistency. Unhappily, as the men at St Andrews, in close cooperation with their friends on the United States Golf Association try to simplify the rules, the more complex they become, but it all adds up to a fascinating situation which is reflected in the nineteenth hole in golf courses round the world where members can regularly be seen poring over and arguing about the rules.

Obviously when you take up the game you will not need to know them off pat and probably will never come across half of them in a lifetime of playing.

KNOW THE BASICS

To gain full enjoyment from the game, however, you would be advised to learn a few of the basic rules, to know what happens when and if you hit out of bounds or into a water hazard, what the penalty is if you hit your opponent's caddy, what happens if you play the wrong ball and so on. That doesn't mean, of course, you have to become one of those rules bores who knows or thinks he knows the ruling for every possible situation and is frequently wrong.

If a snag crops up in a competition round it is easy to check rules with the officials before you sign your card but it is worthwhile carrying a copy of the rules with you in your bag for quick and easy reference. Pocket size copies are readily available from your Club Secretary.

You are allowed to take 14 clubs with you during the round and if by chance you start off with 13 or less you can add clubs to complete the 14 as you play.

If you start with the full complement and break one then you can replace it – as long as the break occurred in the course of playing a shot. If you temperamentally snap your putter across your knee when you miss from two feet or wrap a wedge round an elm tree in temper, well – that is just bad luck. Clubs broken in anger cannot be replaced and that's as it should be. No matter how upset you may be there is no need to break or throw clubs during the round. It's bad manners or, if you like, ungentlemanly conduct but more on that subject later.

If you forget to count your clubs before you start the round and find you have 15 in the bag, you will be penalised two shots for every hole you have played with the additional club in stroke play to a maximum of four strokes and up to a maximum of two holes in match-play, so it is worth doing a spot check on your clubs before you start.

Incidentally, that extra club does not necessarily need to be an adult club as Johnny Miller found out to his amazement and disappointment in the U.S. P.G.A. Championship in 1976. The club he found in his bag was the little 18 inch plastic one his young son had been using two days earlier and which had inadvertently been dropped down into the bottom of the tournament bag.

Although you could argue that Miller clearly had no intention of playing any shots with his son's club, the American P.G.A. decided that the rule regarding extra clubs had been broken and millionaire Miller was penalised.

Personally, I think it was just a little harsh in the circumstances but the Americans run their tour with ruthless rigidity. There are few 'grey' areas, just black or white, when it comes to deciding whether or not to penalise.

Remember then to count your clubs before you start and not to break any in temper as you play round because you will not be able to replace them. Imagine how noted club breaker and thrower Tommy Bolt must have felt when he asked his caddy for an iron to play an approach shot in an American tournament some years ago. The caddy looked somewhat perplexed, then asked, '4 or 9 iron, sir?' They were the only ones left in his bag – or so the story goes!

The teeing area – check that your ball is not tee'd up in front of the markers

Sometimes inadvertently you drive from in front of the markers on the tee, in which case your opponent can ask you to replay your ball in match-play with the first wrong stroke not counting. But in stroke play you must play again, adding two penalty shots to your score. Incidentally, you can play the ball anywhere behind the markers up to a distance of two clublengths. And although the ball must be within the teeing area your stance can be outside.

If, the ball falls off the tee peg as you prepare to drive there is no penalty provided you have not made a stroke at it. Just tee it up again.

The honour in golf is always taken by the player or players who have won the previous hole in match play, or returned the lower score in stroke play, and if, by chance, you do play out of turn you can be asked to replay the shot in match-play, always an annoyance if you have hit a Sunday best drive. There is no penalty for playing out of turn in stroke play.

If you are unlucky enough to lose a ball or hit it out of bounds, the penalty is stroke and distance. You must drop another as close as possible to the spot from which the original shot was hit. You may tee up again if you are hitting a second ball off the tee. If you have to drop a ball remember you are not allowed to throw it down. You must drop it gently over your shoulder as you face the hole so that it does not roll more than two clublengths from the spot at which it is being dropped and no nearer to the hole. If you fail to achieve this at two attempts you may place the ball.

Face the hole when you drop the ball

If you are unlucky enough to lose your ball in the rough you are allowed to look for it for five minutes. If you do not happen to be wearing a watch ask your opponent, or your playing partner, or even an interested spectator to time you. The period of time you search is included in the golf definitions and not in the rules but by common practice that five minute period is now generally accepted as 'the reasonable time' you have before you must declare the ball lost and take alternative action.

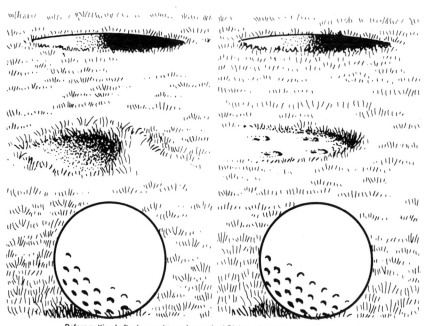

Before putting Left: plug marks can be repaired Right: spike marks cannot be repaired

If your ball lands up in a hazard you are not allowed to touch the sand if it is a bunker or the ground or surface if it is a water hazard. If you do, you will have been deemed to be testing the surface, have taken an unfair advantage and the penalty is a stroke.

Many people wonder just what amount of 'gardening' you can legitimately do when you reach the green. There is provision in the rules for the repair of plug marks – the mark your ball makes when it thuds into the green, and you may also repair spike marks but *not before you have putted.* It could be that spike marks will become repairable under the main rules at some stage in the future but they are not at the moment, so watch you do not step out of line inadvertently.

If you are unlucky enough to come on to a green and find that some heavyweight golfer playing before you has left a dirty great heel mark bang on your putting line, you *cannot* repair it. It may sound a bit unfair but the rules have no provision for you to do so. At all times you may lightly brush aside worm casts, sand, indeed any impediment.

Another rule which causes a certain amount of confusion is the one in which you are, without penalty, allowed to remove natural loose impediments like stones and twigs away from the ball through the green but not in a hazard . . . then there is a penalty.

What confuses the issue here is that you may remove without penalty from a hazard a *non-natural obstruction,* like a cigarette packet or an empty Coke can.

If you wish to seek advice on any shot you may only discuss the matter with your caddy or your partner . . . nobody else. You will be penalised if you or your caddy attempt to gain any advice from 'the opposition' whether you have knowledge of it or not. This happened in the 1971 Ryder Cup when Bernard Gallacher's caddy casually asked Arnold Palmer's caddy what Palmer had hit before Gallacher had played his shot. In this particular instance it was a quite innocent remark but it was overheard by the referee and it cost Gallacher and partner the hole, even allowing for the fact that Gallacher had known nothing about it and had not heard the caddies converse.

If in match-play you hit your caddy or equipment or even yourself with the ball – it may ricochet – you lose the hole just as your opponent loses the hole if he or his caddy or his equipment get in the way of one of your shots. In stroke play, you are penalised two strokes if you hit yourself but your opponent will not be penalised two strokes if *he* or *his* equipment gets in the way of one of your shots. If *you* hit *him* and the

Leave the bunker as you would wish to find it

122

ball bounces badly into an awkward spot then that's a rub of the green. The ball must be played as it lies unless it ends up in your opponent's coat pocket or the 'hit' happens on the green. Then you can replace.

If you play the wrong ball in match play you lose the hole. In stroke play you are penalised two strokes. In both instances there is no penalty for playing the wrong ball in a hazard, provided you find out your mistake and then go on to play the correct ball.

ETIQUETTE

Etiquette is good behaviour and good manners. There are many ways in which you can make the round more enjoyable for those golfers coming behind, and for your partners. Golf is largely like life, a question of imitation – youngsters learn by imitating the swings and habits of their elders. Hopefully if you behave properly your example will be copied by others. Clearly you should keep still when your opponent or your partner is playing. Don't nervously jingle that bunch of keys in your pocket. You may not even hear the sound but your opponent could and might think you were trying to put him off.

Never get in line with a golfer about to putt or stand too close when he is about to play a shot through the green. Move about the course sensibly, giving everyone the best possible chance to play a good shot.

Make sure you always replace your divot after hitting a shot on the fairway even if it means walking a few yards up the fairway to collect the turf. There is nothing more annoying than finding your ball lying in a divot mark made by a previous player who was careless enough or indifferent enough to leave the fairway scar unrepaired!

Always rake the bunkers smooth after you have

Repair your plug marks on the green

played a trap shot. If you have ever come up to a bunker to find your ball nestling in a deep heel mark you will know how exasperating that can be. If there is no rake by the trap – and it is unfortunate these days that rakes are often the target for petty thieves – use your club and shoes to smooth out the surface to the best of your ability.

Move quickly at all times. If you have crawled along behind a tedious four ball you will know just how concentration-sapping a slow round can be and how much enjoyment is lost if you have to wait for every shot. There is no need, for you to run between shots and arrive at the green breathless and unable to putt. Don't rush your actual stroke. Moving quickly on the golf course means moving quickly between shots and not making any undue delay as you weigh up and decide the type of shot you are going to hit, watch where your ball goes and don't expect others to do your job.

If you are unlucky enough to lose your ball don't wait until the five minute search period is almost up before you wave through the players in the following group. Such delays cannot be excused.

Another way to avoid causing unnecessary delay is cross-checking whether or not the golfers coming behind are ready to play their approach shots to the green before you decide to try again the putt that you have just missed. Once you have completed the hole leave the green as quickly as you can. Save yourself unnecessary aggravation and save others time by putting your clubs down at the point most convenient *for the next tee.*

One particularly fast form of golf should be foursomes play but often it is not because the players do not appreciate how to play it. There is no need for you to stay with your partner all the time and watch him play his shot. Since it is alternative shots walk up the fairway to position yourself at the point to which you think your partner will hit. This saves time.

Golf is a game of trust. A golfer walks alone. There is an onus on the golfer to be honest as he plays round and cheating is not only frowned upon, it is just not tolerated. The man (or woman) who cheats is always the loser. If he is caught he will be shunned by his friends – the stigma could last a lifetime. You can be anything but a cheat at golf.

Golf professionals who are convicted of cheating are fined heavily or suspended and any victory you might achieve yourself through even the slightest bit of rule bending will be very hollow indeed. Inadvertent rule breaks happen all the time – mostly on the green – but you must never meaningly break a rule, although at times playing legally within the rules may allow you to take some advantage on the course which you might later consider was morally dishonest.

To illustrate what I mean, you are permitted under the rules to seek relief from an immovable obstruction if it interferes with your stance or swing. Sometimes this relief is only possible if you elect to play away from the hole with the longest club in your bag. Having got relief in this way you are quite entitled then to switch direction and club and hit an 8 iron to the green. It's sharp practice, but it's legal and that is all that matters! Or does it?

In the rough when you are in the rather thick stuff, and your opponent is on the other side of the fairway it would be easy to nudge the ball forward to a better lie . . . but you have your conscience to live with if you do. It is not golf if you do that. The game specifically states you must *play the ball as it lies,* taking the rough with the smooth. If you cannot take it, then you should not be playing golf.

One final point on etiquette. You gain nothing by losing your temper when things are not going right. Banging clubs in the ground, swearing loudly and getting involved in histrionics of any kind will certainly not help your golf and may well upset the people with whom or against whom you are playing. Throwing clubs can be dangerous.

Golf is a character builder. To play your best, to give yourself the best possible chance of doing that you must keep calm and controlled even if you are under considerable pressure. It is all part of the game. Prove to yourself that you are capable of coping and make the game enjoyable for everyone, most of all yourself.

Golf is one of the finest games in the world. Because of its unique handicapping system it is a game between equals. You can start playing when quite young or you can take it up when you are old. If someone wants fresh air and exercise, stimulation and challenge, relaxation and pleasure, my advice is – play golf.

ACKNOWLEDGEMENTS

The photographs are by Keith Hailey and Peter Dazeley
The drawings are by Michael Strand and Graham Webb